Published in the UK in 2013 by Focus Education (UK) Ltd
Updated January 2014

Focus Education (UK) Ltd
Talking Point Conference Centre
Huddersfield Road
Scouthead
Saddleworth
OL4 4AG

Focus Education (UK) Ltd Reg. No 4507968

ISBN 978-1-909038-16-5

Companies, institutions and other organisations wishing to make bulk purchases of books published by Focus Education should contact their local bookstore or Focus Education direct:

Customer Services, Focus Education, Talking Point Conference & Exhibition Centre,
Huddersfield Road, Scouthead, Saddleworth, OL4 4AG
Tel 01457 821818 Fax 01457 878205

www.focus-education.co.uk
customerservice@focus-education.co.uk
Printed in Great Britain by DXG, Manchester

© Focus Education 2014

Focus Education (UK) Ltd: The Team

This new Learning Challenge Curriculum, taking account of the new National Curriculum (2014) has been created by the Focus Education team.

- Clive Davies, Director Focus Education
- Simon Camby, Chief Executive, Focus Academy Trust
- Keith Adams, Focus Education Consultant
- Paul Allen, Teacher, English Martyrs Catholic Primary, Derbyshire
- Jo Davies, Headteacher, Carr Mill Primary, St Helens
- Ros Ferrara, Focus Education Consultant
- Anne McNally, recently retired Headteacher, Wigan
- Tim Nelson, Focus Education Consultant
- Sarah Quinn, Focus Education Consultant
- Helen Rowland, Academy Improvement Officer, Focus Academy Trust

Contents

Note:
All the main areas for each age group have been taken directly from the new National Curriculum. The knowledge, skills and understanding statements come as a result of looking carefully at the requirements for each age group set out in the same documentation.

Introduction

- This scheme of work has been developed to ensure that you will have full coverage of the National Curriculum. It follows the programmes of study for each year very carefully and provides the right balance between using History and Geography as the main drivers but ensuring that creative and expressive arts get a fair representation across the curriculum. They need to be seen alongside the Science Learning Challenges.

- Each set of Learning Challenges then links directly to the History or Geography knowledge, skills and understanding to ensure that learning is progressive and continuous.

- As seen, there has been an attempt to link either creative or expressive arts into each learning challenge so that there is breadth and balance in the coverage as a whole.

- The Art, DT, Music and Dance knowledge, skills and understanding have been taken from the 'Weaving KSU into the new National Curriculum' book which ensures that you will have progression and continuity in these subject areas also.

- The questions outlined in the examples that follow are obviously the starting points for you to consider. The ethos that underpins the Learning Challenge approach requires teachers to check on what children already know and then invite them to think of their own questions. This approach is still highly desirable but teachers need to ensure that they are meeting the National Curriculum requirements. **Very importantly, ensure that all content absolutely meets your context**.

- Each Learning Challenge has a suggested 'wow' and its own suggested reflection. By using these you will get a more complete level of challenge for the pupils.

- You will also note that every opportunity has been taken to help children apply literacy and numeracy skills where it is possible to do so.

- Every attempt has been made to bring History and Geography to life by taking starting points from the children's context. In this way it is hoped that History and Geography will be viewed as exciting and interesting.

- Finally, where a symbol ⬚ is seen it will contain the name and author of a book recommended to be read as a class reader when using the Learning Challenge.

Learning Challenges – The Principles

What are the main principles?

- The Learning Challenge concept is built around the principle of greater learner involvement in their work. It requires deep thinking and encourages learners to work using a question as the starting point.

- In designing the curriculum teachers and learners are using a prime learning challenge, expressed as a question, as the starting point. Using the information gained from pre- learning tasks and the school's context, a series of subsidiary challenges are then planned. Each subsidiary learning challenge is also expressed as a question. See how this works in the schemes of work provided.

- The subsidiary learning challenge is normally expected to last for one week but this does not need to be the case. However, initially it may be useful for the learners and indeed the staff to get used to the weekly learning challenge. The important point is that the learning challenges need to make sense to the learners and be something that is within their immediate understanding.

Learning Challenges – The Principles

How do the Pre- Learning Tasks Work?

- Pre-Learning Tasks ensure that learners are directly involved in the planning process. Well planned pre-learning tasks should help to bring out what learners already know; what misconceptions they may have and what really interests them.

- Teachers should take account of the outcomes from pre-learning tasks to plan the subsidiary learning challenges for each major area of study. It should help teachers recognise which transferable skills learners have already developed that could be used to initiate new learning with a level of confidence.

- Pre-Learning tasks could take many different forms and can last for as long or as short as required. Some may be written tasks, others oral. Mind mapping is one method that has been used successfully by many schools. Using pre-learning tasks as part of a school's programme of home learning will help to get parents and carers directly involved in their children's learning.

The Learning Challenge™
CURRICULUM

Learning Challenges – The Principles

How are learners presented with opportunities to reflect on their learning?

- Time for learners to reflect or review their learning is central to the whole process. This is in keeping with the 'Learning to Learn' principles where reflection is seen as a very important part of individuals' learning programme.

- Within the Learning Challenge Curriculum it is suggested that the final subsidiary learning challenge is handed over for learners to reflect on their learning. The idea is that learners present their learning back to the rest of the class or another appropriate audiemce making the most of their oracy and ICT skills to do so. Initially, learners may require a great deal of direction so the reflection time may need to be presented in the form of a question which helps them to review their work.

- Although reflection is seen as a concluding part of the prime learning challenge, it is hoped that that there will be continual opportunities for learners to reflect frequently, especially as each subsidiary learning challenge comes to an end. Ideally, there should be a good deal of learner autonomy evident during reflection time.

The Learning Challenge™
CURRICULUM

Geography and History Learning Challenges

Year 1

National Curriculum Requirements of Geography at Key Stage 1

Pupils should develop knowledge about the world, the United Kingdom and their locality. They should understand basic subject-specific vocabulary relating to human and physical geography and begin to use geographical skills, including first-hand observation, to enhance their locational awareness.

Pupils should be taught to:

Location knowledge
- name and locate the world's seven continents and five oceans
- name, locate and identify characteristics of the four countries and capital cities of the United Kingdom and its surrounding seas

Place knowledge
- understand geographical similarities and differences through studying the human and physical geography of a small area of the United Kingdom, and of a small area in a contrasting non-European country

Human and physical geography
- identify seasonal and daily weather patterns in the United Kingdom and the location of hot and cold areas of the world in relation to the Equator and the North and South Poles
- use basic geographical vocabulary to refer to:
  - key physical features, including: beach, cliff, coast, forest, hill, mountain, sea, ocean, river, soil, valley, vegetation, season and weather
  - key human features, including: city, town, village, factory, farm, house, office, port, harbour and shop

Geographical skills and fieldwork
- use world maps, atlases and globes to identify the United Kingdom and its countries, as well as the countries, continents and oceans studied at this key stage
- use simple compass directions (North, South, East and West) and locational and directional language (e.g. near and far; left and right) to describe the location of features and routes on a map
- use aerial photographs and plan perspectives to recognise landmarks and basic human and physical features; devise a simple map; and use and construct basic symbols in a key
- use simple fieldwork and observational skills to study the geography of their school and its grounds and the key human and physical features of its surrounding environment.

Pupils should develop an awareness of the past, using common words and phrases relating to the passing of time. They should know where the people and events they study fit within a chronological framework and identify similarities and differences between ways of life in different periods. They should use a wide vocabulary of everyday historical terms. They should ask and answer questions, choosing and using parts of stories and other sources to show that they know and understand key features of events. They should understand some of the ways in which we find out about the past and identify different ways in which it is represented.

Pupils should be taught about:

- changes within living memory. Where appropriate, these should be used to reveal aspects of change in national life
- events beyond living memory that are significant nationally or globally [for example, the Great Fire of London, the first aeroplane flight or events commemorated through festivals or anniversaries]
- the lives of significant individuals in the past who have contributed to national and international achievements. Some should be used to compare aspects of life in different periods [for example, Elizabeth I and Queen Victoria, Christopher Columbus and Neil Armstrong, William Caxton and Tim Berners-Lee, Pieter Bruegel the Elder and LS Lowry, Rosa Parks and Emily Davison, Mary Seacole and/or Florence Nightingale and Edith Cavell]
- significant historical events, people and places in their own locality.

Geography and History Learning Challenges

Year 1

The examples that follow are exactly that, examples.

Consider your context without losing sight of National Curriculum coverage when making adaptations to suit your school and pupils' needs.

Geography and History: Year 1 Overview

	Key Features		
	GEOGRAPHY		**HISTORY**
	Human	**Physical**	
Year 1	• People who live in hot and cold countries • How the seasons and weather affect people	• Features of hot and cold places • Seasonal change • Weather	• Changes within living memory: When parents were young • Significant people from history • Local history
Specific Vocabulary	beach, coast, forest, hill, mountain, ocean, river, soil, valley, vegetation, and weather: city, town, village, factory, farm, house, office, and shop: North, South, East and West; near and far		'before', 'after', 'past', 'present', 'then' and 'now'

Possible Learning Challenges	Why can't a meerkat live in the North Pole?	Where do the leaves go to in winter?	Where do and did the wheels on the bus go?	Why is the Wii more fun than Grandma and Grandad's old toys? or What has changed since your grandparents were young?	Would the Beatles have won X Factor? or Who was famous when mum and dad were little?

Geographical and Historical Knowledge, Skills and Understanding requirements for the National Curriculum

KSU Breakdown – Year1
Geography and History

Knowledge, Skills and Understanding breakdown for History

Year 1

Chronological understanding	Knowledge and interpretation	Historical enquiry
• Can they put up to three objects in chronological order (recent history)? • Can they use words and phrases like: old, new and a long time ago? • Can they tell me about things that happened when they were little? • Can they recognise that a story that is read to them may have happened a long time ago? • Do they know that some objects belonged to the past? • Can they retell a familiar story set in the past? • Can they explain how they have changed since they were born?	• Do they appreciate that some famous people have helped our lives be better today? • Do they recognise that we celebrate certain events, such as bonfire night, because of what happened many years ago? • Do they understand that we have a queen who rules us and that Britain has had a king or queen for many years? • Can they begin to identify the main differences between old and new objects? • Can they identify objects from the past, such as vinyl records?	• Can they ask and answer questions about old and new objects? • Can they spot old and new things in a picture? • Can they answer questions using a artefact/ photograph provided? • Can they give a plausible explanation about what an object was used for in the past?

Year 1 (Challenging)

• Can they put up to five objects/events in chronological order (recent history)? • Can they use words and phrases like: very old, when mummy and daddy were little? • Can they use the words before and after correctly? • Can they say why they think a story was set in the past?	• Can they explain why certain objects were different in the past, e.g. iron, music systems, televisions? • Can they tell us about an important historical event that happened in the past? • Can they explain differences between past and present in their life and that of other children from a different time in history? • Do they know who will succeed the queen and how the succession works?	• Can they answer questions using a range of artefacts/ photographs provided? • Can they find out more about a famous person from the past and carry out some research on him or her?

Knowledge, Skills and Understanding breakdown for Geography

Year 1

Geographical Enquiry	Physical Geography	Human Geography	Geographical Knowledge
• Can they say what they like about their locality? • Can they sort things they like and don't like? • Can they answer some questions using different resources, such as books, the internet and atlases? • Can they think of a few relevant questions to ask about a locality? • Can they answer questions about the weather? • Can they keep a weather chart?	• Can they tell someone their address? • Can they explain the main features of a hot and cold place? • Can they describe a locality using words and pictures? • Can they explain how the weather changes with each season? • Can they name key features associated with a town or village, e.g. 'church', 'farm', 'shop', 'house'?	• Can they begin to explain why they would wear different clothes at different times of the year? • Can they tell something about the people who live in hot and cold places? • Can they explain what they might wear if they lived in a very hot or a very cold place?	• Can they identify the four countries making up the United Kingdom? • Can they name some of the main towns and cities in the United Kingdom? • Can they point out where the equator, north pole and south pole are on a globe or atlas?

Year 1 (Challenging)

Geographical Enquiry	Physical Geography	Human Geography	Geographical Knowledge
• Can they answer questions using a weather chart? • Can they make plausible predictions about what the weather may be like later in the day or tomorrow?	• Can they name key features associated with a town or village, e.g. 'factory', 'detached house', 'semi-detached house', 'terrace house'?	• Can they name different jobs that people living in their area might do?	• Can they name a few towns in the south and north of the UK?

Year 1: Why can't a Meerkat live in the North Pole?

KS1 Geography: identify seasonal and daily weather patterns in the United Kingdom and the location of hot and cold areas of the world in relation to the Equator and the North and South Poles

WOW: Read 'Meerkat Mail'

LC1	Why does Sunny live in the Kalahari desert?
LC2	Which animals live in cold places like the North and South Pole?
LC3	How do Polar Bears keep warm?
LC4	What do we mean by hot and cold colours?
LC5	Why do people usually like going to hot places for their holidays?
LC6	Why do we wear different clothes in summer and winter?
LC7	How can we recreate a Meerkat dance?
LC8	Reflection: Would you rather be a Meerkat or a Penguin?

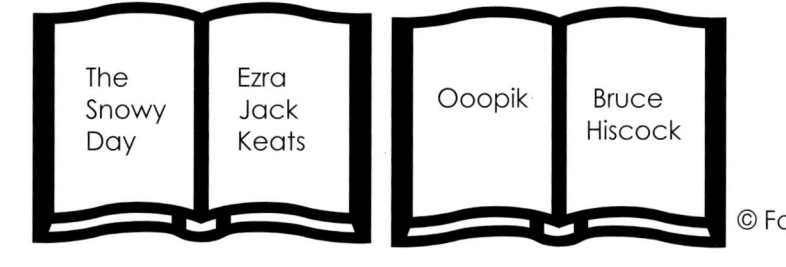

The Snowy Day — Ezra Jack Keats

Ooopik — Bruce Hiscock

Literacy Link:
- Use the book 'Meerkat Mail' to link to postcards sent home from holiday destinations.
- Exciting Vocabulary: equator; poles; centigrade; meerkats; Kalahari; freezing point, etc.

Numeracy Link:
- Possible graphs of children's holiday destinations.
- Consider temperature and how it is measured, create charts from data gathered.

Additional Geography Link:
- Keep an on-going record of the weather in their locality; they could include rainfall, temperature, cloud cover, etc.
- In addition, more able pupils could find out the temperature in certain parts of the world.

Creative Art Link:
- LC4 Mixing paint to create hot and cold paintings.

Expressive Art Link:
- LC7 Movement work focusing on the way Meerkats move. Parents pick up their children 15 minutes early on the Friday so that class can perform to them.

Year 1: Geography Knowledge, Skills and Understanding

Geographical Enquiry	Physical Geography	Human Geography	Geographical Knowledge
• Can they answer some questions using different resources, such as books, the internet and atlases? • Can they think of a few relevant questions to ask about \<a locality>? • Can they answer questions about the weather? • Can they keep a weather chart?	• Can they explain the main features of a hot and cold place? • Can they describe \<a locality> using words and pictures? • Can they explain how the weather changes with each season?	• Can they begin to explain why they would wear different clothes at different times of the year? • Can they say something about the people who live in hot and cold places? • Can they explain what they might wear if they lived in a very hot or a very cold place?	• Can they point out where the Equator, North Pole and South Pole are on a globe or atlas?

Year 1 (Challenging)

• Can they answer questions using a weather chart?
• Can they make plausible predictions about what the weather may be like later in the day or tomorrow?

Year 1 Art & Design Knowledge, Skills and Understanding

Drawing	Painting	Collage	Use of IT
• Can they draw lines of different shapes and thickness?	• Can they name the colours they use, including shades? • Can they create moods in their paintings? • Can they use thick and thin brushes? • Can they name the primary and secondary colours?	• Can they cut and tear paper and card for their collages? • Can they gather and sort the materials they will need?	• Can they use a simple painting program to create a picture? • Can they use tools like fill and brushes in a painting package? • Can they go back and change their picture?

Year 1 Dance Knowledge, Skills and Understanding

- Can they explore and perform basic body actions?
- Do they use different parts of the body singly and in combination?
- Do they show some sense of dynamic, expressive and rhythmic qualities in their own dance?
- Do they choose appropriate movements for different dance ideas?
- Can they remember and repeat short dance phrases and simple dances?
- Do they move with control?
- Do they vary the way they use space?
- Do they describe how their lungs and heart work when dancing?
- Do they describe basic body actions and simple expressive and dynamic qualities of movement?

The Learning Challenge™
CURRICULUM

Year 1: Where do the leaves go to in winter?

KS1 Geography: identify seasonal and daily weather patterns in the United Kingdom

WOW: *Someone comes into the classroom dressed as Mr/s Autumn (leaf suit). Children to prepare questions to ask him or her.*

LC1	Why are there so many leaves on the ground?
LC2	What changes do we see in our country with each season?
LC3	What would you need to do to become the next weather presenter?
LC4	How can you create patterns using leaves in the style of William Morris?
LC5	After listening to music entitled the 'Four Seasons', can you create your own music which captures different weather patterns?
LC6	Why are so many of the things you enjoy doing dependent on the time of year and the weather?
LC7	Reflection: In small groups create a typical weather forecast summary which will be filmed.

Literacy Link: There are many opportunities provided for pupils to develop their oracy skills. These are especially provided within LC3 and during the reflection

Numeracy Link: Lots of opportunity to set things out in charts, especially in relation to the weather. Children will be dealing with centigrade and also measuring rainfall.

Creative Art Link: Having looked at the work of William Morris children should be invited to create their own print and drawing based on the leaves they have found.

Expressive Art Link: There is an opportunity for children to listen to and appreciate classical music.
They will then create their own music based on different elements of weather.

| Lila and the secret of Rain | David Conway & Jude Daly |

The Learning Challenge™
CURRICULUM

Year 1 Geography Knowledge, Skills and understanding

Geographical Enquiry	Physical Geography	Human Geography	Geographical Knowledge
• Can they answer some questions using different resources, such as books, the internet and atlases? • Can they answer questions about the weather? • Can they keep a weather chart?	• Can they explain the main features of a hot and cold place? • Can they explain how the weather changes with each season?	• Can they begin to explain why they would wear different clothes at different times of the year? • Can they say something about the people who live in hot and cold places? • Can they explain what they might wear if they lived in a very hot or a very cold place?	• Can they point out where the equator, north pole and south pole are on a globe or atlas?

Year 1 (Challenging)

• Can they answer questions using a weather chart?
• Can they make plausible predictions about what the weather may be like later in the day or tomorrow?

Year 1 Art & Design Knowledge, Skills and Understanding

Drawing	Printing	Knowledge of Art	Painting
• Can they draw using pencil and crayons? • Can they draw lines of different shapes and thickness, using 2 different grades of pencil?	• Can they print with sponges, vegetables and fruit? • Can they print onto paper and textile? • Can they design their own printing block? • Can they create a repeating pattern?	• Can they describe what they can see and like in the work of another artist? • Can they ask sensible questions about a piece of art?	• Can they choose to use thick and thin brushes as appropriate? • Can they name the primary and secondary colours?

Year 1 Music Knowledge, Skills and Understanding

Performing	Composing	Appraising
• Can they use instruments to perform? • Do they look at their audience when they are performing? • Can they clap short rhythmic patterns? • Can they copy sounds? • Can they make loud and quiet sounds? • Do they know that the chorus keeps being repeated?	• Can they make different sounds with instruments? • Can they identify changes in sounds? • Can they change the sound? • Can they repeat (short rhythmic and melodic) patterns? • Can they make a sequence of sounds? • Can they show sounds by using pictures?	• Can they respond to different moods in music? • Can they say how a piece of music makes them feel? • Can they say whether they like or dislike a piece of music? • Can they choose sounds to represent different things? • Can they recognise repeated patterns?

The Learning Challenge™
CURRICULUM

Year 1: Where do, and did, the wheels on the bus go?

KS1 Geography: use world maps, atlases and globes to identify the United Kingdom and its countries

KS1 History: Pupils should begin to develop an awareness of the past and the ways in which it is similar to and different from the present

WOW: Take a bus tour of the immediate area and go to two contrasting places: village and a town or city.

LC1	Where do we live and what's so special about it?
LC2	How far have you travelled around the United Kingdom?
LC3	How many different ways could you travel around our country?
LC4	Has it always been easy to travel around our country?
LC5	How have cars, buses, trains and bicycles changed since your grandparents were little?
LC6	Can you design and make a vehicle that can move?
LC7	Reflection: Work in groups to put together a presentation on what they know about their country.

Literacy Link: Many opportunities through descriptive writing occur in LC1, LC3, LC5. There are also many opportunities to carry out research about old and new vehicles presented in LC3 and LC4 and 5.

Numeracy Link: There could easily be an opportunity to carry out a traffic survey during LC3.

Creative Art Link: Children will be provided with opportunities to design and make a vehicle in LC6.

Computing Link: During the reflection children should be encouraged to put together a presentation using ICT.

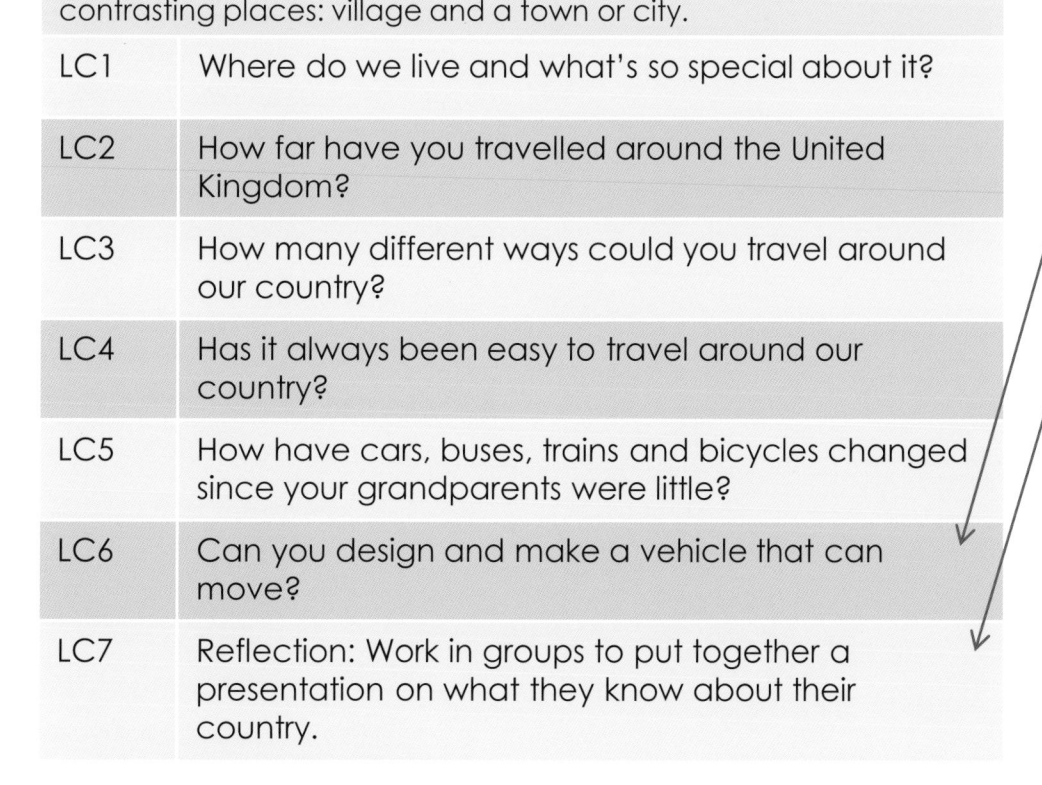

The Naughty Bus   Jan & Jerry Oke

The Learning Challenge™ CURRICULUM

Year 1 Geography Knowledge, Skills and understanding

Geographical Enquiry	Physical Geography	Geographical Knowledge	Challenging
• Can they say what they like about their locality? • Can they sort things they like and don't like? • Can they answer some questions using different resources, such as books, the internet and atlases? • Can they think of a few relevant questions to ask about <a locality>?	• Can they tell someone their address? • Can they describe <a locality> using words and pictures? • Can they name key features associated with a town or village, eg, church, farm, shop, house?	• Can they identify the four countries making up the United Kingdom? • Can they name some of the main towns and cities in the United Kingdom?	• Can they name key features associated with a town or village, eg, factory, detached house, semi-detached house, terrace house? • Can they name a few towns in the south and north of the UK?

Year 1 History Knowledge, Skills and understanding

Chronological understanding	Historical enquiry	Challenging
• Can they put up to three objects in chronological order (recent history)? • Can they use words and phrases like: 'old', 'new' and 'a long time ago'? • Can they tell me about things that happened when they were little? • Can they recognise that a story that is read to them happened a long time ago? • Do they know that some objects belonged to the past?	• Can they ask and answer questions about old and new objects? • Can they spot old and new things in a picture? • Can they answer questions using an artefact/ photograph provided? • Can they give a plausible explanation about what an object was used for in the past?	• Can they begin to identify the main differences between old and new objects? • Can they answer questions using a range of artefacts/ photographs provided?

The Learning Challenge™
CURRICULUM

Year 1 Design Technology Knowledge, Skills and Understanding

Developing, planning and communicating ideas	Working with tools, equipment, materials and components to make quality products	Evaluating processes and products
• Can they think of some ideas of their own? • Can they explain what they want to do? • Can they use pictures and words to plan?	• Can they explain what they are making? • Which tools are they using?	• Can they describe how something works? • Can they talk about their own work and things that other people have done?

Breadth of study

Use of materials	Mechanisms	Construction
• Can they make a structure/model using different materials? • Is their work tidy? • Can they make their model stronger if it needs to be?	• Can they make a product which moves? • Can they cut materials using scissors? • Can they describe the materials using different words? • Can they say why they have chosen moving parts?	• Can they talk with others about how they want to construct their product? • Can they select appropriate resources and tools for their building projects? • Can they make simple plans before making objects, e.g. drawings, arranging pieces of construction before building?

Year 1: Why is the Wii more fun than Grandma and Grandad's old toys?

KS1 History: Changes within living memory - revealing aspects of change in national life

WOW: *Set up 4 Wii consoles in the classroom and invite 6 grandparents to come in and challenge the learners on four different Wii games.*

LC1	Who will win the Wii challenge?
LC2	What was on Grandma and Grandad's Christmas and birthday list?
LC3	Would there have been a Toys R Us around when Grandad was a boy?
LC4	How can you make a moving toy?
LC5	Which toy will you be in Toy Story?
LC6	What would your Christmas have been like without batteries?
LC7	Reflection: Would you choose your toys before your grandparents' toys?

Numeracy Link: Children could keep a record of the points accumulated by each child and grandparent. This could lead to graph work.

Literacy Link: Children could think of a range of questions they would like to ask their grandparents and then interview them. Their recording would be used back in school for research.

Creative Art Link: Opportunities here for children to design and make a moving toy.

Expressive Art Link: Children will perform dances related to toys coming to life.

Science Link: Children will have an opportunity to link with the Science LC 'Why isn't everyone afraid of the dark?'

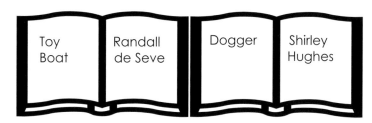

| Toy Boat | Randall de Seve | Dogger | Shirley Hughes |

The Learning Challenge™
CURRICULUM

Year 1: What has changed since my grandparents were young?

KS1 History

Changes within living memory. Where appropriate, these should be used to reveal aspects of change in national life

WOW: *Invite grandparents in to talk to the pupils about their schooldays.*

LC1	What was grandma and grandad's day like at school?
LC2	What sort of phone did our grandparents use?
LC3	Were the Beatles really better than 'One Direction'?
LC4	What sort of television programmes would grandparents have watched?
LC5	Would my grandparents have gone to McDonalds for their birthday parties?
LC6	What would have been on my grandparents' Christmas list?
LC7	What style of clothes would your grandparents have worn when they were your age?
LC8	Reflection: Have all the changes been for the better?

Literacy Link: Children will carry out research on different school days in the 60s (LC1); phones over the past 50 years (LC2). They will also research who the Beatles were and their influence over music in the 60s and 70s

Numeracy Link: Children to work out a time line for various events that are recalled by their grandparents.

Expressive Arts: This LC is linked to appraising and performing a piece of music from the 60s.

Creative Art Link: This LC will see children create sketches from photographs, attempting to capture the fashion of the time.

Did I ever tell you about when your grandparents were young?

Deborah Shaw Lewis & Greg Lewis

The Learning Challenge
CURRICULUM

Year 1 History Knowledge, Skills and Understanding

Chronological understanding	Knowledge and interpretation	Historical enquiry
• Can they put up to three objects in chronological order (recent history)? • Can they use words and phrases like: 'old', 'new' and 'a long time ago'? • Can they tell me about things that happened when they were little? • Do they know that some objects belonged to the past?	• Do they appreciate that some famous people have helped our lives be better today?	• Can they ask and answer questions about old and new objects? • Can they spot old and new objects in a picture? • Can they answer questions using an artefact/ photograph provided? • Can they give a plausible explanation about what an object was used for in the past?
Year 1 (challenging)		
• Can they use words and phrases like: 'very old', 'when mummy and daddy were little'? • Can they use the words 'before' and 'after' correctly? • Can they say why they think a story was set in the past?	• Can they explain why certain objects were different in the past, eg, iron, music systems, televisions? • Can they explain differences between past and present in their life and that of other children from a different time in history?	• Can they begin to identify the main differences between old and new objects? • Can they answer questions using a range of artefacts/ photographs provided? • Can they identify objects from the past, such as vinyl records?

Year 1 Design technology Knowledge, Skills and Understanding

Developing, planning and communicating ideas	Working with tools, equipment, materials and components to make quality products	Evaluating processes and products	Mechanisms
• Can they think of some ideas of their own? • Can they explain what they want to do? • Can they use pictures and words to plan?	• Can they explain what they are making? • Can they explain which tools are they using?	• Can they describe how something works? • Can they talk about their own work and things that other people have done?	• Can they make a product which moves? • Can they cut materials using scissors? • Can they describe the materials using different words? • Can they say why they have chosen moving parts?

Year 1 Dance Knowledge, Skills and Understanding

- Can they explore and perform basic body actions?
- Do they use different parts of the body singly and in combination?
- Do they show some sense of dynamic, expressive and rhythmic qualities in their own dance?
- Do they choose appropriate movements for different dance ideas?
- Can they remember and repeat short dance phrases and simple dances?
- Do they move with control?
- Do they vary the way they use space?
- Do they describe how their lungs and heart work when dancing?
- Do they describe basic body actions and simple expressive and dynamic qualities of movement?

The Learning Challenge™
CURRICULUM

Year 1: Would The Beatles have won 'X Factor'?

KS1 History: the lives of significant individuals in Britain's past who have contributed to our nation's achievements

WOW: Show a brief montage of The Beatles in action and get children to discuss their music in comparison with 'One Direction'.

LC1	Who were The Beatles and why does almost every adult in Britain know them?
LC2	Who else was famous in Britain because of their music?
LC3	If you were in a musical group, what would your music sound like?
LC4	Has Britain always had talent and who would your parents and grandparents say were famous in their day?
LC5	Who are the famous people that have lived in our town/ city/county and what can you find out about them?
LC6	What would you like to become famous for and why?
LC7	Reflection: Can you create a history 'X Factor' show which tells everyone about famous Britons?

Literacy Link: There are many opportunities for children to carry out research. These opportunities should occur during LC1, LC2, LC4 LC5.

Numeracy Link: Opportunities will arise for children to create graphs and tables of favourite musical and other artists. These should occur during LC2, LC3, LC4

Expressive Art Link: During the reflection children should be provided with opportunities to appreciate the talents of others which would almost certainly include appreciation of music.

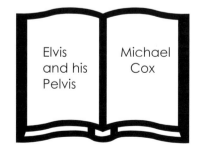

Elvis and his Pelvis

Michael Cox

The Learning Challenge™
CURRICULUM

© Focus Education 2014

29

Year 1: Who was famous when my mum and dad were little?

KS1 History:
the lives of significant individuals in the past who have contributed to national and international achievements.

WOW: *Teacher to deliberately discriminate in favour of children with blue eyes without letting anyone know that they are doing so before getting children to discuss how they felt.*

LC1	What does famous mean and can you find out who your parents would say that they admire?
LC2	Why do we still remember Princess Diana?
LC3	Why was Princess Diana known as 'the people's princess'?
LC4	Who is Nelson Mandela and what would you ask him if you met him?
LC5	How are Nelson Mandela and Princess Diana similar?
LC6	How have famous photographers and artists captured Diana?
LC7	Reflection: What would you like to be famous for and why?

Literacy Link: LC4 provides children with an opportunity to devise their own questions to ask Nelson Mandela.
There are huge opportunities to help develop children's oracy skills, especially in LC1 and LC3 and during the reflection.
LC2 and LC5 provides additional opportunities for children to research about Princess Diana and Nelson Mandela.

Numeracy Link: Opportunities in LC1 for children to collect data and present it in a variety of forms.

Creative Art Link: LC6 provides children with an opportunity to find out the work of other artists and then to create their own self-portrait using the media that they have been looking at.

Peaceful Protest   Yona Zeldis McDonough

Year 1 History Knowledge, Skills and Understanding

Chronological understanding	Knowledge and interpretation	Historical enquiry
• Can they put up to three objects in chronological order (recent history)? • Can they use words and phrases like: 'old', 'new' and 'a long time ago'? • Can they tell me about things that happened when they were little? • Can they recognise that a story that is read to them happened a long time ago? • Do they know that some objects belonged to the past? • Can they retell a familiar story set in the past? • Can they explain how they have changed since they were born?	• Do they understand that we have a queen who rules us and that Britain has had a king or queen for many years? • Do they appreciate that some famous people have helped our lives be better today?	• Can they ask and answer questions about old and new objects? • Can they spot old and new things in a picture? • Can they answer questions using an artefact/ photograph provided? • Can they give a plausible explanation about what an object was used for in the past?
Year 1 (challenging)		
• Can they put up to five objects/events in chronological order (recent history)? • Can they use words and phrases like: 'very old', 'when mummy and daddy were little'? • Can they use the words 'before' and 'after' correctly? • Can they say why they think a story was set in the past?	• Can they explain why certain objects were different in the past, eg, iron, music systems, televisions? • Can they tell us about an important historical event that happened in the past? • Can they explain differences between past and present in their life and that of other children from a different time in history?	• Can they begin to identify the main differences between old and new objects? • Can they answer questions using a range of artefacts/ photographs provided? • Can they identify objects from the past, such as vinyl records? • Can they find out more about a famous person from the past and carry out some research on him or her?

Geography and History Learning Challenges

Year 2

The examples that follow are exactly that, examples.

Consider your context without losing sight of National Curriculum coverage when making adaptations to suit your school and pupils' needs.

Geography and History: Year 2 Overview

Key Features				
	GEOGRAPHY		**HISTORY**	
	Human	**Physical**		
Year 2	• a small area of the United Kingdom, and of a small area in a contrasting non-European country • identify seasonal and daily weather patterns in the United Kingdom • use simple fieldwork and observational skills to study the geography of their school and its grounds and the key human and physical features of its surrounding environment.		• Changes and events beyond living memory that are significant nationally or globally • significant historical events, people and places in their own locality • significant people from Britain or abroad	
Specific Vocabulary	beach, coast, forest, hill, mountain, ocean, river, soil, valley, vegetation, and weather: city, town, village, factory, farm, house, office, and shop: North, South, East and West: near and far		'before', 'after', 'past', 'present', 'then' and 'now'	
Possible Learning Challenges	What would Dora the Explorer/ Ben Ten find exciting about our town/city?	Why do we love to be beside the seaside?	Where would you prefer to live: England or Africa?	What were the people who lived here like a 100 years ago? or What was it like when the Queen came to the throne in 1953?	How have Rosa Parks and Nelson Mandela helped to make the world a better place? Why were Christopher Columbus and Neil Armstrong brave people?

Geographical and Historical Knowledge, Skills and Understanding requirements for the National Curriculum

KSU Breakdown – Year 2
Geography and History

Knowledge, Skills and Understanding breakdown for History

Year 2

Chronological understanding

- Can they use words and phrases like: before I was born, when I was younger?
- Can they use phrases and words like: 'before', 'after', 'past', 'present', 'then' and 'now'; in their historical learning?
- Can they use the words 'past' and 'present' accurately?
- Can they use a range of appropriate words and phrases to describe the past?
- Can they sequence a set of events in chronological order and give reasons for their order?

Knowledge and interpretation

- Can they recount the life of someone famous from Britain who lived in the past giving attention to what they did earlier and what they did later?
- Can they explain how their local area was different in the past?
- Can they recount some interesting facts from an historical event, such as where the 'Fire of London' started?
- Can they give examples of things that are different in their life from that of their grandparents when they were young?
- Can they explain why Britain has a special history by naming some famous events and some famous people?
- Can they explain what is meant by a parliament?

Historical enquiry

- Can they find out something about the past by talking to an older person?
- Can they answer questions by using a specific source, such as an information book?
- Can they research the life of a famous Briton from the past using different resources to help them?
- Can they research about a famous event that happens in Britain and why it has been happening for some time?
- Can they research the life of someone who used to live in their area using the Internet and other sources to find out about them?

Year 2 (Challenging)

- Can they sequence a set of objects in chronological order and give reasons for their order?
- Can they sequence events about their own life?
- Can they sequence events about the life of a famous person?
- Can they try to work out how long ago an event happened?

- Can they give examples of things that are different in their life from that of a long time ago in a specific period of history such as the Victorian times?
- Can they explain why someone in the past acted in the way they did?
- Can they explain why their locality (as wide as it needs to be) is associated with a special historical event?
- Can they explain what is meant by a democracy and why it is a good thing?

- Can they say at least two ways they can find out about the past, for example using books and the internet?
- Can they explain why eye-witness accounts may vary?
- Can they research about a famous event that happens somewhere else in the world and why it has been happening for some time?

Knowledge, Skills and Understanding breakdown for Geography

Year 2

Geographical Enquiry	Physical Geography	Human Geography	Geographical Knowledge
• Can they label a diagram or photograph using some geographical words? • Can they find out about a locality by using different sources of evidence? • Can they find out about a locality by asking some relevant questions to someone else? • Can they say what they like and don't like about their locality and another locality like the seaside?	• Can they describe some physical features of their own locality? • Can they explain what makes a locality special? • Can they describe some places which are not near the school? • Can they describe a place outside Europe using geographical words? • Can they describe some of the features associated with an island? • Can they describe the key features of a place, using words like, beach, coast forest, hill, mountain, ocean, valley?	• Can they describe some human features of their own locality, such as the jobs people do? • Can they explain how the jobs people do may be different in different parts of the world? • Do they think that people ever spoil the area? How? • Do they think that people try to make the area better? How? • Can they explain what facilities a town or village might need?	• Can they name the continents of the world and find them in an atlas? • Can they name the world's oceans and find them in an atlas? • Can they name the major cities of England, Wales, Scotland and Ireland? • Can they find where they live on a map of the UK?

Year 2 (Challenging)

Geographical Enquiry	Physical Geography	Human Geography	Geographical Knowledge
• Can they make inferences by looking at a weather chart? • Can they make plausible predictions about what the weather may be like in different parts of the world?	• Can they find the longest and shortest route using a map? • Can they use a map, photographs, film or plan to describe a contrasting locality outside Europe?	• Can they explain how the weather affects different people?	• Can they locate some of the world's major rivers and mountain ranges? • Can they point out the North, South, East and West associated with maps and compass?

Year 2: What would *Dora the Explorer* find exciting about our town/city?

KS1 Geography: use simple fieldwork and observational skills to study the geography of their school and its grounds and the key human and physical features of its surrounding environment.

WOW: *Children receive a visit from Dora or Ben and they need to have a range of questions to ask them about where they want to visit.*

LC1	Where could I take *Dora on a special outing in our town?
LC2	Why would *Dora need to know my postcode to find my house?
LC3	Where could I take *Dora for a special holiday in the United Kingdom?
LC4	How would *Dora use her map to find her way to school?
LC5	What would appear on *Dora's map of our town?
LC6	How can we create paintings from our photographs of special places in our town?
LC7	Reflection: How could Dora use our town in one of her TV adventures?

Literacy Link: Children will have to think of a number of questions they would ask Dora if she appeared in their classroom.

Numeracy Link: Links with addresses and number.

Creative Art Link: Children will take photographs of famous landmarks/ buildings in their town and then look at the work of a range of artists before creating their own painting/ drawing.

Follow That Map

Scot Ritchie

N.B. *Dora could be replaced by any well-known character that all your class are familiar with. Dora has good geographical links because of her association with maps.

Year 2 Geography Knowledge, Skills and Understanding

Geographical Enquiry	Physical Geography	Human Geography	Geographical Knowledge
• Can they label a diagram or photograph using some geographical words? • Can they find out about their town by using different sources of evidence? • Can they find out about their town by asking some relevant questions to someone else? • Can they say what they like and don't like about their locality and another locality like the seaside?	• Can they describe some physical features of their town? • Can they explain what makes their town special? • Can they describe some places which are not near the school? • Can they describe the key features of a place, using words like, 'forest', 'hill', 'mountain', 'valley'?	• Can they describe some human features of their town, such as the jobs people do? • Do they think that people ever spoil the area? How? • Do they think that people try to make the area better? How? • Can they explain what facilities a town or village might need?	• Can they find where they live on a map of the UK?

Year 2 (Challenging)

- Can they find the longest and shortest route using a map?
- Can they use a map, photographs, film or plan to describe <a contrasting locality> outside Europe?
- Can they point out the North, South, East and West associated with maps and compass?

Year 2 Art & Design Knowledge, Skills and Understanding

Painting	Drawing	Knowledge	Sketch Books
• Can they mix paint to create all the secondary colours? • Can they mix and match colours, predict outcomes? • Can they mix their own brown? • Can they make tints by adding white? • Can they make tones by adding black?	• Can they use three different grades of pencil in their drawing (4B, 8B, HB)? • Can they use charcoal, pencil and pastels? • Can they create different tones using light and dark? • Can they show patterns and texture in their drawings? • Can they use a viewfinder to focus on a specific part of an artefact before drawing it?	• Can they say how other artists have used colour, pattern and shape? • Can they create a piece of work in response to another artist's work?	• Can they begin to demonstrate their ideas through photographs and in their sketch books? • Can they set out their ideas, using 'annotation' in their sketch books? • Do they keep notes in their sketch books as to how they have changed their work?

The Learning Challenge™
CURRICULUM

Year 2: Why do we love to be beside the seaside?

KS1 Geography: identify seasonal and daily weather patterns in the United Kingdom
— human and physical features of a small area of the United Kingdom

WOW: *A visit to a local seaside resort.*

LC1	Where do you go to on holiday and why?
LC2	What attracts visitors to seaside resorts?
LC3	What do you notice about the coast and how is it different to your town?
LC4	What can we learn about lifeboats and lighthouses?
LC5	What was *Blackpool* like in the past?
LC6	Can you create your own digital postcards?
LC7	What can you find in rock pools?
LC7	Reflection: Working in groups children will create a presentation on 'What makes a seaside special?'

Literacy Link: Opportunities in LC3 for descriptive writing and further opportunities in LC5 and 6 for research and postcard style writing.

Numeracy Link: LC1 provides opportunities for children to carry out research about their favourite holiday destinations and create graphs and charts

Creative Arts Link: LC2 provides opportunities for children to design and make a fairground ride similar to that found by the seaside.

Creative Art Link: LC6 provides opportunities for children to take photographs when on their visit and then use these photographs to create their own postcard.

Science Links: Opportunities here to link with science work in LC4 and LC7.

N.B. *Blackpool mentioned here but replace *Blackpool with your own seaside destination.

Billy's Bucket — Kes Gray & Garry Parsons

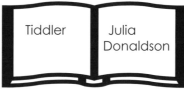

Tiddler — Julia Donaldson

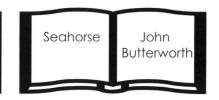

Seahorse — John Butterworth

The Learning Challenge™ **CURRICULUM**

Year 2 Geography Knowledge, Skills and Understanding

Geographical Enquiry	Physical Geography	Human Geography	Geographical Knowledge
• Can they label a diagram or photograph using some geographical words? • Can they find out about the seaside by using different sources of evidence? • Can they find out about the seaside by asking some relevant questions to someone else? • Can they say what they like and don't like about their locality and another locality like the seaside?	• Can they describe some physical features of own locality? • Can they explain what makes the seaside special? • Can they describe some of the features associated with an island? • Can they describe the key features of a place, using words like, 'beach', 'coast', 'forest', 'hill', 'mountain', 'ocean', 'valley'?	• Can they describe some human features of the seaside, such as the jobs people do? • Can they explain how the jobs people do may be different in different parts of the world? • Do they think that people ever spoil the area? How? • Do they think that people try to make the area better? How? • Can they explain what facilities a town or village might need?	• Can they name the major cities of England, Wales, Scotland and Ireland? • Can they find where they live on a map of the UK?

Year 2 (Challenging)

• Can they find the longest and shortest route using a map?
• Can they explain how the weather affects different people?
• Can they point out the North, South, East and West associated with maps and compass?

Year 2 Design Technology Knowledge, Skills and Understanding

- Can they think of ideas and plan what to do next?
- Can they choose the best tools and materials? Can they give a reason why these are best?
- Can they describe their design by using pictures, diagrams, models and words?
- What went well with their work?
- If they did it again, what would they want to improve?
- Can they make sensible choices as to which material to use for their constructions?
- Can they develop their own ideas from initial starting points?
- Can they incorporate some type of movement into models?
- Can they consider how to improve their construction?
- Can they measure materials to use in a model or structure?
- Can they join material in different ways?
- Can they use joining, folding or rolling to make it stronger?

Year 2: Where would you prefer to live: England or Africa?

KS1 Geography: understand geographical similarities and differences through studying the human and physical geography of a small area of the United Kingdom, and of a contrasting non-European country.
Identify seasonal and daily weather patterns in the United Kingdom and the location of hot and cold areas of the world

WOW: *A visit from African dancers or drummers*

LC1	What would you ask …………?
LC2	What are *African people proud of?
LC3	What are the main differences in the climate of *Africa and England?
LC4	Which animals would you find living in the wild in *Africa?
LC5	How can you recreate *African art?
LC6	Do *Africans live a healthier life than we do?
LC7	What would your school day be like if you lived in *Africa?
LC8	Can you recreate *African music?
LC9	Reflection: Can the class create an *African exhibition.

Literacy Link: LC1 requires children to think of a range of questions they would wish to ask a visitor from Africa (these may be members of a dance or music group invited to school or could be a local person who has strong connections with Africa.
In addition LC2, LC3 and LC4 enables children to carry out research and develop writing opportunities as a result.

Creative Art Link: Children to look at the colour associated with African artists such as Martin Bulinya and recreate their own paintings in an African style.

Expressive Art Link: Children would be encouraged to listen to the rhythms associated with African music and try to recreate their own music giving consideration to the choice of instruments and their voices.

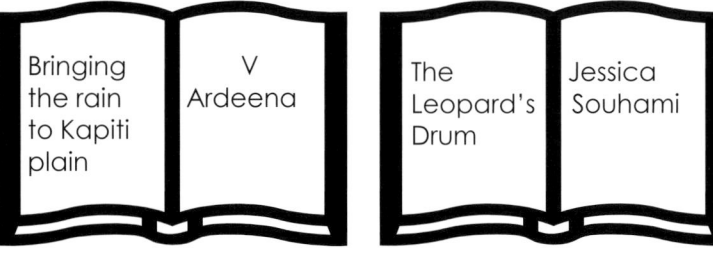

Bringing the rain to Kapiti plain	V Ardeena	The Leopard's Drum	Jessica Souhami

Although *Africa is mentioned here it would be preferable to look at a specific African country such as Kenya.

Year 2 Geography Knowledge, Skills and Understanding

Geographical Enquiry	Physical Geography	Human Geography	Geographical Knowledge
• Can they label a diagram or photograph using some geographical words? • Can they find out about a contrasting locality like Africa by using different sources of evidence? • Can they find out about Africa by asking some relevant questions to someone else? • Can they say what they like and don't like about their locality and another locality like Africa?	• Can they explain what makes a locality special? • Can they describe a place outside Europe using geographical words? • Can they describe the key features of a place, using words like, 'beach', 'coast', 'forest', 'hill', 'mountain', 'ocean', 'valley'?	• Can they explain how the jobs people do may be different in different parts of the world? • Do they think that people ever spoil the area? How? • Do they think that people try to make the area better? How?	• Can they name the continents of the world and find them in an atlas? • Can they name the world's oceans and find them in an atlas?
Year 2 (Challenging)			
• Can they make plausible predictions about what the weather may be like in different parts of the world?	• Can they find the longest and shortest route using a map? • Can they use a map, photographs, film or plan to describe Africa?	• Can they explain how the weather affects different people?	• Can they locate some of the world's major rivers and mountain ranges? • Can they point out the North, South, East and West associated with maps and compass?

Year 2 Art & Design Knowledge, Skills and Understanding

Drawing	Painting	Knowledge	Sketch books
• Can they use three different grades of pencil in their drawing (4B, 8B, HB)? • Can they use charcoal, pencil and pastels? • Can they create different tones using light and dark? • Can they show patterns and texture in their drawings? • Can they use a viewfinder to focus on a specific part of an artefact before drawing it?	• Can they mix paint to create all the secondary colours? • Can they mix and match colours and predict outcomes? • Can they mix their own brown? • Can they make tints by adding white? • Can they make tones by adding black?	• Can they link colours to natural and man-made objects? • Can they say how other artists have used colour, pattern and shape? • Can they create a piece of work in response to another artist's work?	• Can they begin to demonstrate their ideas through photographs and in their sketch books? • Can they set out their ideas, using 'annotation' in their sketch books? • Do they keep notes in their sketch books as to how they have changed their work?

Year 2 Music Knowledge, Skills and Understanding

- Can they listen out for particular things when listening to music?
- Can they order sounds to create a beginning, middle and end?
- Can they create music in response to <different starting points>?
- Can they choose sounds which create an effect?
- Can they use symbols to represent sounds?
- Can they make connections between notations and musical sounds?

The Learning Challenge™
CURRICULUM

Year 2: What was it like when the Queen came to the throne in 1953?

KS1 History: events beyond living memory that are significant nationally or globally

WOW: *Children to carry out a mock coronation giving particular attention to the key events in a coronation.*

LC1	What is a coronation and what does one look like?
LC2	What would you have done after school if you had lived in 1953?
LC3	What would your favourite football team have looked like in 1953? Or, What would your favourite dress have looked like in 1953?
LC4	What was the British Empire?
LC5	What key events have happened since the Queen has reigned?
LC6	What job does the Queen do?
LC7	How much would our shopping basket have cost in 1953?
LC8	Reflection: Children to put together a presentation to do with our monarchy.

Literacy Link: Opportunities for children to role play a coronation and develop oracy skills during LC1. Additional opportunities for research provided through LC2, LC3, LC4 and LC6.

Numeracy Link: Great opportunity provided in LC5 for linking dates with events and in LC7 for developing number skills through money.

Creative Arts Link: Children could research in the first instance and then design their own football team kit based around this time or they could design a special dress that might have been worn at this time.

Additional Geography Link: Children to use maps to find out about the location of countries within the British Empire and at the same time locate continents and oceans on their maps.

The Learning Challenge
CURRICULUM

Year 2 History Knowledge, Skills and Understanding

Chronological understanding	Knowledge and interpretation	Historical enquiry
• Can they use words and phrases like: *'before I was born'*, *'when I was younger'*? • Can they use phrases and words like: 'before', 'after', 'past', 'present', 'then' and 'now'; in their historical learning? • Can they use the words 'past' and 'present' correctly? • Can they use a range of appropriate words and phrases to describe the past?	• Can they recount the life of someone famous from Britain who lived in the past, giving attention to what they did earlier and what they did later? • Can they give examples of things that are different in their life from that of their grandparents when they were young? • Can they explain why Britain has a special history by naming some famous events and some famous people? • Can they explain what is meant by a parliament?	• Can they find out something about the past by talking to an older person? • Can they answer questions by using a specific source, such as an information book? • Can they research the life of a famous Briton from the past using different resources to help them? • Can they research about a famous event that happens in Britain and why it has been happening for some time?

Year 2 (Challenging)

• Can they sequence a set of events in chronological order and give reasons for their order? • Can they sequence a set of objects in chronological order and give reasons for their order? • Can they sequence events about their own life? • Can they try to work out how long ago an event happened?	• Can they give examples of things that are different in their life from that of a long time ago in a specific period of history such as 1953? • Can they explain why their locality (as wide as it needs to be) is associated with a special historical event? • Can they explain what is meant by a democracy and why it is a good thing?	• Can they say at least two ways they can find out about the past, for example using books and the internet? • Can they explain why eye-witness accounts may vary?

Year 2 Additional Geography Knowledge, Skills and Understanding

• Can they name the continents of the world and find them in an atlas?
• Can they name the world's oceans and find them in an atlas?
• Can they name the major cities of England, Wales, Scotland and Ireland?
• Can they find where they live on a map of the UK?

The Learning Challenge™
CURRICULUM

Year 2: What were the people who lived in *our town like a 100 years ago?

KS1 History: events beyond living memory that are significant nationally or globally	
WOW: *Take a planned walk around the locality and decide what was and was not there 100 years ago*	
LC1	What can your grandparents tell you?
LC2	What can we learn about the past by looking at photographs and artefacts?
LC3	What would it have been like to have gone to school 100 years ago?
LC4	What do you think you would have been doing on Saturdays and Sundays 100 years ago?
LC5	Can you create a game that you may have played 100 years ago?
LC6	Are there any famous pieces of music that were played or sung 100 years ago?
LC7	Reflection: Children to create a presentation 'A day in my life 100 years ago.'

Literacy Link: LC1 provides children with an opportunity to devise their own questions to ask their grandparents.

Numeracy Link: There will be continual opportunities for children to link events to dates and work out 'how long ago'. This is especially the case for LC2.

Creative Art Link: LC5 provides children with an opportunity to design and make a game that could have been played 100 years ago. This could be a board game or a playground game.

Expressive Art Link: LC6 gives children a chance to learn some traditional English songs and to perform them. These would include choral speaking opportunities.

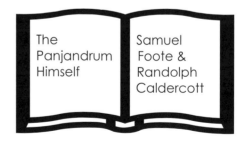

The Panjandrum Himself

Samuel Foote & Randolph Caldercott

*Our town in this learning challenge should be replaced by your nearest named town, city or even village.

Year 2 History Knowledge, Skills and Understanding

Chronological understanding	Knowledge and interpretation	Historical enquiry
• Can they use words and phrases like: *'before I was born'*, *'when I was younger'*? • Can they use phrases and words like: 'before', 'after', 'past', 'present', 'then' and 'now'; in their historical learning? • Can they use the words 'past' and 'present' correctly? • Can they use a range of appropriate words and phrases to describe the past?	• Can they recount the life of someone famous from Britain who lived in the past, giving attention to what they did earlier and what they did later? • Can they recount some interesting facts from an historical event? • Can they give examples of things that are different in their life from that of their grandparents when they were young? • Can they explain why Britain has a special history by naming some famous events and some famous people?	• Can they find out something about the past by talking to an older person? • Can they answer questions by using a specific source, such as an information book? • Can they research the life of a famous Briton from the past using different resources to help them? • Can they research about a famous event that happens in Britain and why it has been happening for some time?

Year 2 (Challenging)

• Can they sequence a set of events in chronological order and give reasons for their order? • Can they sequence a set of objects in chronological order and give reasons for their order? • Can they sequence events about their own life? • Can they sequence events about the life of a famous person? • Can they try to work out how long ago an event happened?	• Can they give examples of things that are different in their life from that of a long time ago in a specific period of history, e.g. 100 years ago? • Can they explain why someone in the past acted in the way they did? • Can they explain how their local area was different in the past? • Can they explain why their locality (as wide as it needs to be) is associated with a special historical event? • Can they explain what is meant by a democracy and why it is a good thing?	• Can they say at least two ways they can find out about the past, for example using books and the internet? • Can they explain why eye-witness accounts may vary? • Can they research the life of someone who used to live in their area using the Internet and other sources to find out about them? • Can they research about a famous event that happens somewhere else in the world and why it has been happening for some time?

Year 2 Design Technology Knowledge, Skills and Understanding

Developing, planning and communicating ideas	Working with tools, equipment, materials and components to make quality products	Evaluating processes and products	Use of materials
• Can they think of ideas and plan what to do next? • Can they choose the best tools and materials? Can they give a reason why these are best? • Can they describe their design by using pictures, diagrams, models and words?	• Can they join things (materials/ components) together in different ways?	• What went well with their work? • If they did it again, what would they want to improve?	• Can they measure materials to use in a model or structure? • Can they join material in different ways? • Can they use joining, folding or rolling to make it stronger?

Year 2 Music Knowledge, Skills and Understanding

• Do they sing and follow the melody (tune)?
• Do they sing accurately at a given pitch?
• Can they perform simple patterns and accompaniments keeping a steady pulse?
• Can they perform with others?
• Can they sing/clap a pulse increasing or decreasing in tempo?
• Can they listen out for particular things when listening to music?

The Learning Challenge™
CURRICULUM

Year 2: How have Rosa Parks and Nelson Mandela helped to make the world a better place?

KS1 History: the lives of significant individuals in the past who have contributed to national and international achievements.

WOW: *Teacher to deliberately discriminate in favour of children with blue eyes without letting anyone know that they are doing so before getting children to discuss how they felt.*

LC1	What do you understand by the word 'discrimination'?
LC2	Who was Rosa Parks and who was Nelson Mandela and why should we be proud of them?
LC3	Do you think that children discriminate in any way?
LC4	What can you find out about slavery and why was it such a bad thing?
LC5	What can you find out about non-British music and art?
LC6	What can you find out about the American President Obama?
LC7	Reflection: Children to perform plays that help others see how wrong it is to discriminate.

Literacy Link: LC2 provides children with an opportunity to devise their own questions to ask Rosa Parks and Nelson Mandela.
There are huge opportunities to help develop children's oracy skills, especially in LC3 and during the reflection.
LC4 and LC6 provides additional opportunities for children to research about President Obama and slavery.

Creative Art Link: LC5 provides children with an opportunity to find out and recreate art from another culture.

Expressive Art Link: LC5 also gives children a chance to learn about the music traditionally associated with black people.

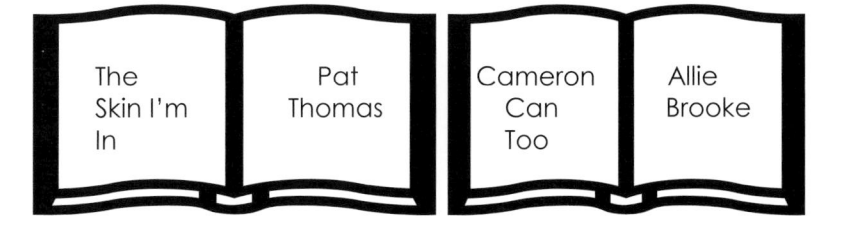

The Skin I'm In   Pat Thomas   Cameron Can Too   Allie Brooke

Year 2: Why were Christopher Columbus and Neil Armstrong very brave people?

KS1 History: the lives of significant individuals in Britain's past who have contributed to our nation's achievements

WOW: Have a spaceman and a pirate appear in the classroom and the children could prepare questions to ask them

LC1	What would we need to take with us on a voyage of discovery?
LC2	Who was Christopher Columbus and why do we talk about him today?
LC3	What would it be like to be a spaceman?
LC4	Who do you know that's famous and what can you find about them?
LC5	Can you create a space painting or a painting of an old ship sailing on the sea?
LC6	Why would Christopher Columbus's voyages have been very dangerous?
LC7	How did Christopher Columbus and Neil Armstrong make our world a better place?
LC8	Reflection: What would you like to become famous for and why?

Literacy Link: There are many opportunities for children to carry out research. These opportunities should occur during LC2, LC3 and LC4.

Numeracy Link: Opportunities will arise for children to create graphs and tables of favourite musical and other artists. These should occur during LC2, LC3, LC4

Creative Art Link: Children will be asked to look at photographs taken from space and of the work of famous painters such as Turner and try to create their own painting based on one of these two themes.

On The Moon — Anna Milbourne & Benji Davies

The Pirate Cruncher — Jonny Duddle

The Learning Challenge™
CURRICULUM

Year 2 History Knowledge, Skills and Understanding breakdown

Chronological understanding	Knowledge and interpretation	Historical enquiry
• Can they use words and phrases like: *'before I was born'*, *'when I was younger'*? • Can they use phrases and words like: 'before', 'after', 'past', 'present', 'then' and 'now'; in their historical learning? • Can they use the words 'past' and 'present' correctly? • Can they use a range of appropriate words and phrases to describe the past? • Can they sequence a set of events in chronological order and give reasons for their order?	• Can they recount the life of someone famous from outside Britain who lived in the past giving attention to what they did earlier and what they did later? • Can they recount some interesting facts from an historical event?	• Can they find out something about the past by talking to an older person? • Can they answer questions by using a specific source, such as an information book? • Can they research the life of a famous non-Briton from the past using different resources to help them?
Year 2 (Challenging)		
• Can they sequence a set of objects in chronological order and give reasons for their order? • Can they sequence events about the life of a famous person? • Can they try to work out how long ago an event happened?	• Can they explain why someone in the past acted in the way they did? • Can they explain what is meant by a democracy and why it is a good thing?	• Can they say at least two ways they can find out about the past, for example using books and the internet? • Can they explain why eye-witness accounts may vary? • Can they research about a famous event that happens somewhere else in the world and why it has been happening for some time?

The Learning Challenge™
CURRICULUM

Year 2 Art & Design Knowledge, Skills and Understanding breakdown

Drawing	Painting	Knowledge	Sketch books
• Can they use three different grades of pencil in their drawing (4B, 8B, HB)? • Can they use charcoal, pencil and pastels? • Can they create different tones using light and dark? • Can they show patterns and texture in their drawings?	• Can they mix paint to create all the secondary colours? • Can they mix and match colours, predict outcomes? • Can they mix their own brown? • Can they make tints by adding white? • Can they make tones by adding black?	• Can they link colours to natural and man-made objects? • Can they say how other artists have used colour, pattern and shape? • Can they create a piece of work in response to another artist's work?	• Can they begin to demonstrate their ideas through photographs and in their sketch books? • Can they set out their ideas, using 'annotation' in their sketch books? • Do they keep notes in their sketch books as to how they have changed their work?

Year 2 Music Knowledge, Skills and Understanding breakdown

- Can they perform simple patterns and accompaniments keeping a steady pulse?
- Can they perform with others?
- Can they play simple rhythmic patterns on an instrument?
- Can they sing/clap a pulse increasing or decreasing in tempo?
- Can they create music in response to <different starting points>?
- Can they choose sounds which create an effect?
- Can they use symbols to represent sounds?
- Can they make connections between notations and musical sounds?

Geography and History Learning Challenges

Key Stage 1 Examples taking account of local contexts

The examples that follow are exactly that, examples.

Consider your context without losing sight of National Curriculum coverage when making adaptations to suit your school and pupils' needs.

Year 1: What are the differences between Leigh and the rainforests?

KS1 Geography:
Understand geographical similarities and differences through studying the human and physical geography of a small area of the United Kingdom, and of a small area in a contrasting non-European country.

WOW: Look at two filmed clips of a domestic pet and a wild animal (preferably cats)and talk about the main differences.

LC1	What do the homes of people who live in Leigh look like?
LC2	How would you go about building a shelter to survive a few days in the Rainforests?
LC3	Why do plants grow to be so big in the rainforests?
LC4	What do we mean by camouflage and why is it important for some of the animals who live in the rainforest to be able to camouflage themselves?
LC5	What can you find out about one of the animals that lives in the rainforest?
LC6	How can you compare the temperature and the rainfall in the rainforest and in Leigh at different times of the year?
LC8	Can you take turns to present a filmed presentation of your work on this LC?

Literacy Link:
LC5 provides opportunities for pupils to engage in research about one animal that they want to find out more about. They will need to use the internet and information books to source their evidence.

Numeracy Link:
- Possible graphs about rainfall and temperature.

Additional Science Link:
- LC3 provides opportunities for children to consider what plants need to grow and to look at the impact that extreme heat and rain has on plants.

Creative Art Link:
- LC2 Provides opportunities for children to design their own shelters and to make them to a simple scale.

The Shaman's Apprentice — Lynne Cherry

The Rainforest Grew all Around — Susan K Mitchell

Year 2: Why did the Titanic sink?

KS1 History:
a significant event beyond living memory.

WOW: *Children to be awarded a ticket to go on a special journey.*

LC1	What was the Titanic and why do we talk about it today?
LC2	What can you find out about some of the people who were on board?
LC3	How can you recreate the events of the sinking of the Titanic?
LC4	How can you recreate a model of the Titanic?
LC5	Which type of music and dances did the passengers enjoy?
LC6	How long does it take for an iceberg to melt?
LC7	What was different about being a first or a third class passenger?
LC8	Reflection: Can you create your own simulation of the sinking of the Titanic and film it?

Literacy Link: LC2 provides opportunities for children to research and find out about particular people that were on board the Titanic.

Creative Art Link: LC4 provides children with an opportunity to find out about the Titanic and to recreate a model using accurate observations. They could also create the ocean by investigating different media.

Expressive Art Link: LC5 also gives children a chance to learn about the music traditionally associated with this period in history and to link the dances they did with the TV programme 'Strictly Come Dancing'.

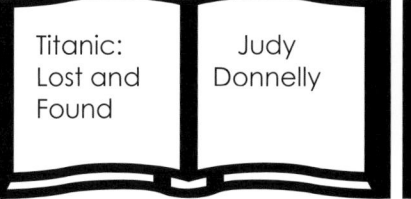

Titanic: Lost and Found
Judy Donnelly

Story of The Titanic
Steve Noon

The Learning Challenge™
CURRICULUM

Geography and History Learning Challenges

Key Stage 2

National Curriculum Requirements of Geography at Key Stage 2

Pupils should extend their knowledge and understanding beyond the local area to include the United Kingdom and Europe, North and South America. This will include the location and characteristics of a range of the world's most significant human and physical features. They should develop their use of geographical knowledge, understanding and skills to enhance their locational and place knowledge.

Pupils should be taught to:

Location knowledge
- locate the world's countries, using maps to focus on Europe (including the location of Russia) and North and South America, concentrating on their environmental regions, key physical and human characteristics, countries, and major cities
- name and locate counties and cities of the United Kingdom, geographical regions and their identifying human and physical characteristics, key topographical features (including hills, mountains, coasts and rivers), and land-use patterns; and understand how some of these aspects have changed over time
- identify the position and significance of latitude, longitude, Equator, Northern Hemisphere, Southern Hemisphere, the Tropics of Cancer and Capricorn, Arctic and Antarctic Circle, the Prime/Greenwich Meridian and time zones (including day and night)

Place knowledge
- understand geographical similarities and differences through the study of human and physical geography of a region of the United Kingdom, a region in a European country, and a region within North or South America

Human and physical geography
describe and understand key aspects of:
- physical geography, including: climate zones, biomes and vegetation belts, rivers, mountains, volcanoes and earthquakes, and the water cycle
- human geography, including: types of settlement and land use, economic activity including trade links, and the distribution of natural resources including energy, food, minerals and water

Geographical skills and fieldwork
- use maps, atlases, globes and digital/computer mapping to locate countries and describe features studied
- use the eight points of a compass, four and six-figure grid references, symbols and key (including the use of Ordnance Survey maps) to build their knowledge of the United Kingdom and the wider world
- use fieldwork to observe, measure, record and present the human and physical features in the local area using a range of methods, including sketch maps, plans and graphs, and digital technologies.

National Curriculum Requirements of History at Key Stage 2

Pupils should continue to develop a chronologically secure knowledge and understanding of British, local and world history, establishing clear narratives within and across the periods they study. They should note connections, contrasts and trends over time and develop the appropriate use of historical terms. They should regularly address and sometimes devise historically valid questions about change, cause, similarity and difference, and significance. They should construct informed responses that involve thoughtful selection and organisation of relevant historical information. They should understand how our knowledge of the past is constructed from a range of sources.

In planning to ensure the progression described above through teaching the British, local and world history outlined below, teachers should combine overview and depth studies to help pupils understand both the long arc of development and the complexity of specific aspects of the content.

Pupils should be taught about:

changes in Britain from the Stone Age to the Iron Age
Examples (non-statutory)
This could include:
- late Neolithic hunter-gatherers and early farmers, for example, Skara Brae
- Bronze Age religion, technology and travel, for example, Stonehenge
- Iron Age hill forts: tribal kingdoms, farming, art and culture

the Roman Empire and its impact on Britain
Examples (non-statutory)
This could include:
- Julius Caesar's attempted invasion in 55-54 BC
- the Roman Empire by AD 42 and the power of its army
- successful invasion by Claudius and conquest, including Hadrian's Wall
- British resistance, for example, Boudica
- 'Romanisation' of Britain: sites such as Caerwent and the impact of technology, culture and beliefs, including early Christianity

In planning to ensure the progression described above through teaching the British, local and world history outlined below, teachers should combine overview and depth studies to help pupils understand both the long arc of development and the complexity of specific aspects of the content.

Pupils should be taught about:

Britain's settlement by Anglo-Saxons and Scots
Examples (non-statutory)
This could include:
- Roman withdrawal from Britain in c. AD 410 and the fall of the western Roman Empire
- Scots invasions from Ireland to north Britain (now Scotland)
- Anglo-Saxon invasions, settlements and kingdoms: place names and village life
- Anglo-Saxon art and culture
- Christian conversion – Canterbury, Iona and Lindisfarne

the Viking and Anglo-Saxon struggle for the kingdom of England to the time of Edward the Confessor
Examples (non-statutory)
This could include:
- Viking raids and invasion
- resistance by Alfred the Great and Athelstan, first king of England
- further Viking invasions and Danegeld
- Anglo-Saxon laws and justice
- Edward the Confessor and his death in 1066

Pupils should continue to develop a chronologically secure knowledge and understanding of British, local and world history, establishing clear narratives within and across the periods they study. They should note connections, contrasts and trends over time and develop the appropriate use of historical terms. They should regularly address and sometimes devise historically valid questions about change, cause, similarity and difference, and significance. They should construct informed responses that involve thoughtful selection and organisation of relevant historical information. They should understand how our knowledge of the past is constructed from a range of sources.

In planning to ensure the progression described above through teaching the British, local and world history outlined below, teachers should combine overview and depth studies to help pupils understand both the long arc of development and the complexity of specific aspects of the content.

Pupils should be taught about:

a local history study
Examples (non-statutory)
- a depth study linked to one of the British areas of study listed above
- a study over time tracing how several aspects of national history are reflected in the locality (this can go beyond 1066)
- a study of an aspect of history or a site dating from a period beyond 1066 that is significant in the locality.

a study of an aspect or theme in British history that extends pupils' chronological knowledge beyond 1066
Examples (non-statutory)
- the changing power of monarchs using case studies such as John, Anne and Victoria
- changes in an aspect of social history, such as crime and punishment from the Anglo-Saxons to the present or leisure and entertainment in the 20th Century
- the legacy of Greek or Roman culture (art, architecture or literature) on later periods in British history, including the present day
- a significant turning point in British history, for example, the first railways or the Battle of Britain

- **the achievements of the earliest civilizations** – an overview of where and when the first civilizations appeared and a depth study of one of the following: Ancient Sumer; The Indus Valley; Ancient Egypt; The Shang Dynasty of Ancient China

- **Ancient Greece** – a study of Greek life and achievements and their influence on the western world

- **a non-European society** that provides contrasts with British history – one study chosen from: early Islamic civilization, including a study of Baghdad c. AD 900; Mayan civilization c. AD 900; Benin (West Africa) c. AD 900-1300.

History breakdown – Key Stage 2

A simplistic overview of history coverage in Key Stage 2 is outlined below. However, this is just one interpretation and is in no way meant to be the only way of looking at coverage.

	Stone Age to 1066	Ancient Civilizations	Significant Themes in British history (Preferably from a Local interest point of view)	
Year 3	**Changes in Britain from the Stone Age to the Iron Age**	**(Coverage in any Year group)**	**Examples**	
Year 4	**The Roman Empire and its impact on Britain**	• **Ancient Greece** **One of:** • Ancient Sumer • Ancient Egypt • Indus Valley • Shang Dynasty **One of:** • Mayan Civilization C900 • Early Islamic Civilization c900 • Benin (West Africa) c900 - 1300	• Henry VIII – Break from the RC Church • World War 2 – Battle of Britain • Norman Conquest – feudal system • Gunpowder, treason and plot – Charles 1 execution	• Crime and Punishment – Anglo Saxons to today (Who were the early lawmakers?) • Leisure and entertainment in the 20th century • What the Greeks or Romans do for our cultures, art and literature
Year 5	**Britain's settlement by Anglo-Saxons and Scots**			
Year 6	**The Viking and Anglo-Saxon struggle for the kingdom of England to the time of Edward the Confessor**			

The following Year 3 to Year 6 examples are provided as a guide only. There is no compulsion to keep to any year group and therefore rolling programmes for mixed aged classes and schools with small numbers are very possible. The document 'Weaving Knowledge, Skills and Understanding within the new National Curriculum' (see website guide) will provide progression and continuity for pupils and staff. Page 167 provides an alternative view by combining the chronology into one Learning Challenge. This opens more opportunities for greater choice from the right hand side column on this page.

Geography and History Learning Challenges

Year 3

The examples that follow are exactly that, examples.

Consider your context without losing sight of National Curriculum coverage when making adaptations to suit your school and pupils' needs.

Geography and History: Year 3 Overview

	Key Features				
	GEOGRAPHY		**HISTORY**		
	Human	**Physical**			
Year 3	**European Country** • holiday destination • famous cities	**Volcanoes, Earthquakes and Tsunamis** • The power of the Earth	**Stone Age to the Iron Age,** including: • Hunter gatherers • Early farming • Bronze Age, and • Iron Age	**Ancient Greece** • A study of Greek life and achievements and their influence on the western world	**Local History** • A study of Local History taking account of a period of history that shaped the locality
Learning Challenges	Why do so many people choose to go to the Mediterranean for their holidays?	What makes the Earth angry?	Who first lived in Britain?	Why has Greece always been in the news?	*How did the Victorian period help to shape the Atherton we know today? *Do you think Sir Titus Salt was a hero or a villain?

The Local History Learning Challenge will need to reflect a period of time that has meaning for your locality. However, some of the LC questions used in the example might help you with framing your weekly Learning Challenges.

Geographical and Historical Knowledge, Skills and Understanding requirements for the National Curriculum

KSU Breakdown – Year 3
Geography and History

Knowledge, Skills and Understanding breakdown for History

Year 3

Chronological understanding	Knowledge and interpretation	Historical enquiry
• Can they describe events and periods using the words: BC, AD and decade? • Can they describe events from the past using dates when things happened? • Can they describe events and periods using the words: ancient and century? • Can they use a timeline within a specific time in history to set out the order things may have happened? • Can they use their mathematical knowledge to work out how long ago events would have happened?	• Do they appreciate that the early Brits would not have communicated as we do or have eaten as we do? • Can they begin to picture what life would have been like for the early settlers? • Can they recognise that Britain has been invaded by several different groups over time? • Do they realise that invaders in the past would have fought fiercely, using hand to hand combat? • Can they suggest why certain events happened as they did in history? • Can they suggest why certain people acted as they did in history?	• Do they recognise the part that archaeologists have had in helping us understand more about what happened in the past? • Can they use various sources of evidence to answer questions? • Can they use various sources to piece together information about a period in history? • Can they research a specific event from the past? • Can they use their 'information finding' skills in writing to help them write about historical information? • Can they, through research, identify similarities and differences between given periods in history?

Year 3 (Challenging)

• Can they set out on a timeline, within a given period, what special events took place? • Can they begin to recognise and quantify the different time periods that exists between different groups that invaded Britain?	• Can they begin to appreciate why Britain would have been an important country to have invaded and conquered? • Can they appreciate that war/s would inevitably have brought much distress and bloodshed? • Do they have an appreciation that wars start for specific reasons and can last for a very long time? • Do they appreciate that invaders were often away from their homes for very long periods and would have been 'homesick'?	• Can they begin to use more than one source of information to bring together a conclusion about an historical event? • Can they use specific search engines on the Internet to help them find information more rapidly?

Knowledge, Skills and Understanding breakdown for Geography

Year 3

Geographical Enquiry	Physical Geography	Human Geography	Geographical Knowledge
• Do they use correct geographical words to describe a place and the events that happen there? • Can they identify key features of a locality by using a map? • Can they begin to use 4 figure grid references? • Can they accurately plot NSEW on a map? • Can they use some basic OS map symbols? • Can they make accurate measurement of distances within 100Km?	• Can they use maps and atlases appropriately by using contents and indexes? • Can they describe how volcanoes are created? • Can they describe how earthquakes are created? • Can they confidently describe physical features in a locality? • Can they locate the Mediterranean and explain why it is a popular holiday destination? • Can they recognise the 8 points of the compass (N,NW, W, S, SW, SE, E, NE)?	• Can they describe how volcanoes have an impact on people's lives? • Can they confidently describe human features in a locality? • Can they explain why a locality has certain human features? • Can they explain why a place is like it is? • Can they explain how the lives of people living in the Mediterranean would be different from their own?	• Can they name a number of countries in the Northern Hemisphere? • Can they locate and name some of the world's most famous volcanoes? • Can they name and locate some well-known European countries? • Can they name and locate the capital cities of neighbouring European countries? • Are they aware of different weather in different parts of the world, especially Europe?

Year 3 (Challenging)

• Can they work out how long it would take to get to a given destination taking account of the mode of transport?	• Can they explain why a locality has certain physical features?	• Can they explain how people's lives vary due to weather?	• Can they name the two largest seas around Europe?

Year 3: What makes the Earth angry?

KS2 Geography: pupils to be taught physical geography, including: climate zones, biomes and vegetation belts, rivers, mountains, volcanoes and earthquakes, and the water cycle

WOW: *Show a range of clips from Tsunami; volcanoes and hurricane. Video conference a school in Iceland.*

LC1	What causes a volcano to erupt and which are the famous volcanoes in the world?
LC2	How do volcanoes impact on the lives of people and why do people choose to live near them?
LC3	How can we recreate an erupting volcano?
LC4	What causes an earthquake (and a tsunami) and how are they measured?
LC5	Who experiences extreme weather in our country?
LC6	Which countries have experienced earthquakes and tsunamis in your life time?
LC7	How can we capture a stormy weather pattern using music, drama and dance?
LC8	Reflection: Each group to put together a weather presentation of extreme weather using music, drama and video clips.

Literacy Link: During LC1 the children will be asked to research volcanoes in the world and pin point them onto a world map.
During LC2 children will asked to think of a range of questions they would like to ask an Icelandic child. These will be emailed or asked during a video conferencing session.
During LC4 the children will be asked to research earthquakes and tsunamis and write about them in a Learning Challenge journal.
During LC5 children will link with children who have experienced flooding. Again opportunities could be made for video conferencing or emailing (children in Japan).

Creative Art Link: During LC3 children will be provided with an opportunity to design and make a volcano and then they will need to think of a way of making it erupt.

Numeracy Link: LC4 provides opportunities for scale work.

Expressive Art Link: During LC7 there will be opportunities for children to create some music which will be used as part of their reflection presentations. Possibly Peter Grimes.

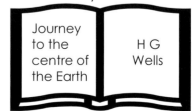

Journey to the centre of the Earth — H G Wells

The Learning Challenge™ CURRICULUM

Year 3 Geography Knowledge, Skills and Understanding

Geographical Enquiry	Physical Geography	Human Geography	Geographical Knowledge
• Do they use correct geographical words to describe a place and the things that happen there? • Can they identify key features of a locality by using a map? • Can they make accurate measurement of distances within 100Km?	• Can they use maps and atlases appropriately by using contents and indices? • Can they describe how volcanoes are created? • Can they describe how earthquakes are created? • Can they confidently describe physical features in a locality?	• Can they describe how volcanoes have an impact on people's lives? • Can they confidently describe human features in a locality? • Can they explain why a locality has certain human features?	• Can they name a number of countries in the Northern and Southern Hemisphere? • Can they locate and name some of the world's most famous volcanoes? • Can they name and locate some well-known European countries? • Are they aware of different weather in different parts of the world, especially Europe?
Year 3 (Challenging)			
• Can they work out how long it would take to get to a given destination taking account of the mode of transport?	• Can they explain why a locality has certain physical features?	• Can they explain how people's lives vary due to weather?	• Can they name the two largest seas around Europe?

Year 3 Design Technology Knowledge, Skills and Understanding

Developing, planning and communicating ideas	Working with tools, equipment, materials and components to make quality products	Evaluating processes and products	Mouldable materials
• Can they show that their design meets a range of requirements? • Can they put together a step-by-step plan which shows the order and also what equipment and tools they need? • Can they describe their design using an accurately labelled sketch and words? • How realistic is their plan?	• Can they use equipment and tools accurately?	• What did they change which made their design even better?	• Do they select the most appropriate materials? • Can they use a range of techniques to shape and mould? • Do they use finishing techniques?

Year 3 Music Knowledge, Skills and Understanding

• Can they create repeated patterns with different instruments?
• Can they create accompaniments for tunes?
• Can they combine different sounds to create a specific mood or feeling?
• Can they improve their work; explaining how it has improved?
• Can they use musical words (the elements of music) to describe a piece of music and compositions?
• Can they use musical words to describe what they like and dislike?
• Can they recognise the work of at least one famous composer?

The Learning Challenge™
CURRICULUM

Year 3: Why do so many people go to the Mediterranean for their holidays?

KS2 Geography: understand geographical similarities and differences through the study of human and physical geography of a region or area of the United Kingdom and a region or area in a European country

WOW: A visit to or from a travel agent having thought of questions to ask first.

LC1	What are the advantages/ disadvantages of living in a Mediterranean country?
LC2	Why do Mediterranean countries have a warmer climate than we do?
LC3	Which fruits and vegetables are produced in the Mediterranean?
LC4	How can we organise a Mediterranean food festival?
LC5	How would you go about attracting someone to visit a Mediterranean country?
LC6	Why doesn't everyone speak English and use the same money?
LC7	Who are the famous artists of the Mediterranean and what can we learn from them?
LC8	Which European cities can we associate with different types of music?
LC9	Reflection: Children in groups choose a European city and put together a special presentation as part of a European day in school (holiday programme style).

Literacy Link: LC1 provides opportunities for explanation text and opportunities for different ways of presenting information.
In LC5 children will have to make use of their persuasive skills to entice people to their chosen city.

Numeracy Link: LC3 provides opportunities for children to weigh and measure fruits as well as collect data about favourite fruit etc.

Creative Art Link: There are opportunities in LC4 and the reflection for children to design and make a Mediterranean food dish.
In addition,
LC7 provides opportunities for children to paint in the style of a well-known Mediterranean artist.

Expressive Art Link: LC8 provides opportunities for children to consider the famous musicians of Europe and to listen to their works. This can range from Liverpool's Beatles to the Viennese waltzes.

The Mystery of the Mona Lisa

Elizabeth Singer Hunt

The Learning Challenge™ **CURRICULUM**

Year 3 Geography Knowledge, Skills and Understanding

Geographical Enquiry	Physical Geography	Human Geography	Geographical Knowledge
• Do they use correct geographical words to describe a place and the things that happen there? • Can they identify key features of a locality by using a map? • Can they use some basic OS map symbols? • Can they make accurate measurement of distances within 100Km?	• Can they use maps and atlases appropriately by using contents and indexes? • Can they confidently describe physical features in a locality? • Can they locate the Mediterranean and explain why it is a popular holiday destination?	• Can they confidently describe human features in a locality? • Can they explain why a locality has certain human features? • Can they explain why a place is like it is? • Can they explain how the lives of people living in the Mediterranean would be different from their own?	• Can they name some well-known European countries? • Can they name and locate the capital cities of neighbouring European countries? • Are they aware of different weather in different parts of the world, especially Europe?

Year 3 Food Technology Knowledge, Skills and Understanding

Cooking and Nutrition
- Can they choose the right ingredients for a product?
- Can they use equipment safely?
- Can they make sure that their product looks attractive?
- Can they describe how their combined ingredients come together?
- Can they set out to grow plants such as cress and herbs from seed with the intention of using them for their food product?
- Can they show that their design meets a range of requirements?
- Can they put together a step-by-step plan which shows the order and also what equipment and tools they need?
- Can they describe their design using an accurately labelled sketch and words?
- How realistic is their plan?
- Can they use equipment and tools accurately?
- What did they change which made their design even better?

The Learning Challenge™
CURRICULUM

Year 3 Art & Design Knowledge, Skills and Understanding

Drawing	Painting	Knowledge	Sketch books
• Can they use their sketches to produce a final piece of work? • Can they write an explanation of their sketch in notes? • Can they use different grades of pencil shade, to show different tones and texture?	• Can they predict with accuracy the colours that they mix? • Do they know where each of the primary and secondary colours sits on the colour wheel? • Can they create a background using a wash? • Can they use a range of brushes to create different effects?	• Can they compare the work of different artists? • Can they explore work from other cultures? • Can they explore work from other periods of time? • Are they beginning to understand the viewpoints of others by looking at images of people and understand how they are feeling and what the artist is trying to express in their work?	• Can they use their sketch books to express feelings about a subject and to describe likes and dislikes? • Can they make notes in their sketch books about techniques used by artists? • Can they suggest improvements to their work by keeping notes in their sketch books?

Year 3 Music Knowledge, Skills and Understanding

- Can they improve their work; explaining how it has improved?
- Can they use musical words (the elements of music) to describe a piece of music and compositions?
- Can they use musical words to describe what they like and dislike?
- Can they recognise the work of at least one famous composer?

Year 3: Has Greece always been in the news?

KS2 Geography: understand geographical similarities and differences through the study of human and physical geography of a region or area in a European country;
KS2 History: A study of Greek life and achievements and their influence on the western world

WOW: *Visit from a Greek warrior, dressed accordingly, with expectation that children already have questions ready of him.*

LC1	Where is Greece and why do so many people enjoy going on holiday there?
LC2	How do Greece's physical features, including its climate differ from ours?
LC3	How does Greece's climate impact on its people?
LC4	Who were the Ancient Greeks and what did we learn from them?
LC5	How would a tourist to Greece today be reminded of the power of the Ancient Greeks?
LC6	...and the Oscar goes to? (Which Greek God would you choose to receive a special award?)
LC7	Would you have enjoyed being an Olympian?
LC8	What is democracy and what part did the Greeks have in creating it?
LC9	How would you go about reproducing a clay pot in the style of the Greeks?
LC10	Reflection: Children to put on a special Greek event for parents to include features of ancient and modern Greece.

Literacy Link: LC6 presents opportunities for children to find out information about one of the Greek Gods.
LC8 provides opportunities for children to debate issues and to understand more about democracy.
LC5 provides children with opportunities to research the main tourist attractions in Greece.

Numeracy Link: Opportunities in LC1 for children to carry out surveys and to present information in data and statistical forms.

Creative Art Link: The children should research how the Greeks made clay pots and use techniques such as coiling to make their own and decorate them accordingly.

Men And Gods — Rex Warner

Ancient Greece — Linda Honan

The Learning Challenge™ CURRICULUM

Year 3 History Knowledge, Skills and Understanding

Chronological understanding	Knowledge and interpretation	Historical enquiry
• Can they describe events from the past using dates when things happened? • Can they describe events and periods using the words: ancient and century? • Can they use a timeline within a specific time in history to set out the order things may have happened? • Can they use their mathematical knowledge to work out how long ago events would have happened?	• Do they realise that invaders in the past would have fought fiercely, using hand to hand combat? • Do they appreciate that wars have happened from a very long time ago and are often associated with invasion, conquering or religious differences? • Can they suggest why certain events happened as they did in history? • Can they suggest why certain people acted as they did in history?	• Can they use various sources of evidence to answer questions? • Can they use various sources to piece together information about a period in history? • Can they research a specific event from the past ? • Can they use their 'information finding' skills in writing to help them write about historical information? • Can they, through research, identify similarities and differences between given periods in history?

Year 3 (Challenging)

• Can they set out on a timeline, within a given period, what special events took place?	• Can they appreciate that war/s would inevitably have brought much distress and bloodshed? • Do they have an appreciation that wars start for specific reasons and can last for a very long time? • Do they appreciate that invaders were often away from their homes for very long periods and would have been 'homesick'?	• Can they begin to use more than one source of information to bring together a conclusion about an historical event? • Can they use specific search engines on the Internet to help them find information more rapidly?

The Learning Challenge™
CURRICULUM

Year 3 Geography Knowledge, Skills and Understanding

Geographical Enquiry	Physical Geography	Human Geography	Geographical Knowledge
• Do they use correct geographical words to describe a place and the things that happen there? • Can they identify key features of a locality by using a map? • Can they make accurate measurement of distances within 100Km?	• Can they use maps and atlases appropriately by using contents and indices? • Can they confidently describe physical features in a locality? • Can they locate the Mediterranean and explain why it is a popular holiday destination?	• Can they confidently describe human features in a locality? • Can they explain why a locality has certain human features? • Can they explain how the lives of people living in the Mediterranean would be different from their own?	• Can they name a number of countries in the Northern Hemisphere? • Can they name and locate some well-known European countries? • Can they name and locate the capital cities of neighbouring European countries? • Are they aware of different weather in different parts of the world, especially Europe?

Year 3 (Challenging)

• Can they work out how long it would take to get to a given destination taking account of the mode of transport?	• Can they explain why a locality has certain physical features?	• Can they explain how people's lives vary due to weather?	• Can they name the two largest seas around Europe?

Year 3 Art Knowledge, Skills and Understanding

• Can they begin to sculpt clay and other mouldable materials?
• Can they use specific clay techniques to create a pot?

© Focus Education 2014

Year 3: Who first lived in Britain?

KS2 History: Stone Age to the Iron Age, including:
- Hunter gatherers; Early farming; Bronze Age, and Iron Age

WOW: *Share a presentation about the artefacts found related to the Ancient Britons and consider their purposes.*
Visit to an archaeologist site (if possible).

LC1	What jobs do archaeologists do and why are they so valuable in helping us find out about history?
LC2	How did the Early Britons make shelters?
LC3	Would the Early Britons have visited a supermarket for their food?
LC4	What can you find out about the Stone, Bronze and Iron Ages?
LC5	What do we know about the life styles of the early Britons through the art they produced?
LC6	What do we know about the way they moved heavy items around?
LC7	How do you think the early Britons would have communicated?
LC8	Reflection: Working in groups the children should put together a ICT presentation of the life of Early Britons taking account of their weapons, food, ways of communicating and eating.

Literacy Link: Opportunities for children to carry out research exist in LC1, LC2, LC3 and LC4.

Literacy Link: In LC4 the children will divide into 3 groups with each group researching one of the ages mentioned. They will then create a presentation to each other.

Creative Art Link: In LC2 children will design and make their own model shelters based on what they have found out from researching the shelters of the early Britons.

Creative Art Link: LC5 provides opportunities for children to experiment with their own art having first researched the art of the Ancient Britons.

Science Links: Opportunities here for children to experiment with finding ways of moving heavy objects.

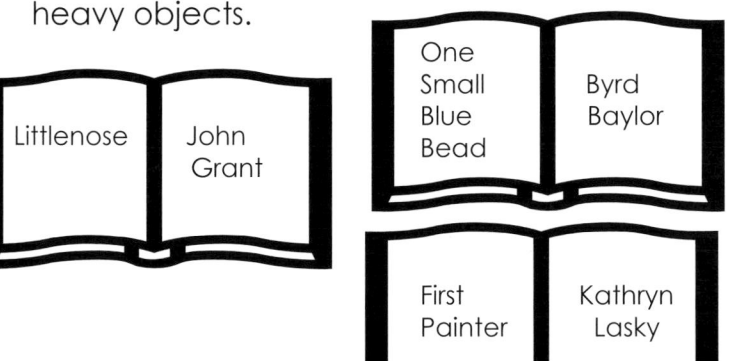

Littlenose John Grant

One Small Blue Bead Byrd Baylor

First Painter Kathryn Lasky

The Learning Challenge™ CURRICULUM

Year 3 History Knowledge, Skills and Understanding

Chronological understanding	Knowledge and interpretation	Historical enquiry
• Can they describe events from the past using dates when things happened? • Can they describe events and periods using the words: ancient and century? • Can they use a timeline within a specific time in history to set out the order things may have happened? • Can they use their mathematical knowledge to work out how long ago events would have happened?	• Can they recognise that Britain has been invaded by several different groups over time? • Do they realise that invaders in the past would have fought fiercely, using hand to hand combat? • Do they appreciate that wars have happened from a very long time ago and are often associated with invasion, conquering or religious differences?	• Can they use various sources of evidence to answer questions? • Can they use various sources to piece together information about a period in history? • Can they research a specific event from the past ? • Can they use their 'information finding' skills in writing to help them write about historical information?

Year 3 (Challenging)

• Can they set out on a timeline, within a given period, what special events took place?	• Do they have an appreciation that wars start for specific reasons and can last for a very long time?	• Can they begin to use more than one source of information to bring together a conclusion about an historical event? • Can they use specific search engines on the Internet to help them find information more rapidly?

Year 3 Art & Design Knowledge, Skills and Understanding

- Can they use their sketches to produce a final piece of work?
- Can they write an explanation of their sketch in notes?
- Can they use different grades of pencil shade, to show different tones and texture?
- Can they predict with accuracy the colours that they mix?
- Do they know where each of the primary and secondary colours sits on the colour wheel?
- Can they use a range of brushes to create different effects?
- Can they use their sketch books to express feelings about a subject and to describe likes and dislikes?
- Can they make notes in their sketch books about techniques used by artists?
- Can they suggest improvements to their work by keeping notes in their sketch books?
- Can they explore work from other cultures?
- Can they explore work from other periods of time?

Year 3 Design Technology Knowledge, Skills and Understanding

- Can they show that their design meets a range of requirements?
- Can they put together a step-by-step plan which shows the order and also what equipment and tools they need?
- Can they describe their design using an accurately labelled sketch and words?
- Can they assess how realistic their plan is?
- Can they use equipment and tools accurately?
- What did they change which made their design even better?
- Do they use the most appropriate materials?
- Can they work accurately to make cuts and holes?
- Can they join materials?

Year 3: How did the Victorian period help to shape the Atherton we know today?

KS2 History: Local History - A study of Local History taking account of a period of history that shaped the locality

WOW: Children to go on a guided walk through a part of Atherton and photograph what was there 100 years ago; between 50 and 100 years ago; and less than 50 years ago.

LC1	What made people come and live in Atherton in the first place?
LC2	When did St. Richard's Church and school open and what can we find out about their history?
LC3	Why does Atherton have a Pitt memorial?
LC4	Has anyone famous ever lived in Atherton?
LC5	How can we capture Atherton's history in art and music?
LC6	What is Enamill and why is it an important part of the history of Atherton?
LC7	Why does Atherton have a railway station and when was it opened?
LC8	Reflection: Children to carry out an IT presentation of the advantages and disadvantages of living in Victorian Atherton

Literacy Link: Opportunities for children to carry out research exist in LC1, LC2, LC3, LC4, LC6 and LC7.

Literacy Link: In LC2 the children will divide into 2 groups with each group researching the history of the school or the history of the Church.

Creative Art Link: In LC5 half the children will use old photographs and create their own images of Atherton based on LS Lowry's style. The other half can look at Atherton today and paint the buildings in the same street as the Lowry group.

Expressive Art Links: Children will perform the music that children would have sung in Victorian times

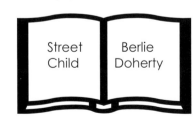

Street Child — Berlie Doherty

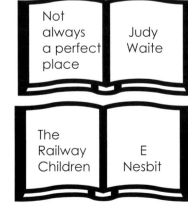

Not always a perfect place — Judy Waite

The Railway Children — E Nesbit

Year 3 History Knowledge, Skills and Understanding breakdown

Chronological understanding	Knowledge and interpretation	Historical enquiry
• Can they describe events from the past using dates when things happened? • Can they use a timeline within a specific period in history to set out the order events may have happened? • Can they use their mathematical knowledge to work out how long ago events would have happened?	• Can they suggest why certain events happened as they did in history? • Can they suggest why certain people acted as they did in history?	• Can they use various sources of evidence to answer questions? • Can they use various sources to piece together information about a period in history? • Can they research a specific event from the past ? • Can they use their 'information finding' skills in writing to help them write about historical information? • Can they, through research, identify similarities and differences between given periods in history?

Year 3 (Challenging)

• Can they set out on a timeline, within a given period, what special events took place?
• Can they begin to use more than one source of information to bring together a conclusion about an historical event?
• Can they use specific search engines on the Internet to help them find information more rapidly?

Knowledge, Skills and Understanding breakdown for Art and Music

Art & Design	Music
• Can they use their sketches to produce a final piece of work? • Can they write an explanation of their sketch in notes? • Can they use different grades of pencil shade, to show different tones and texture? • Can they predict with accuracy the colours that they mix? • Do they know where each of the primary and secondary colours sits on the colour wheel? • Can they create a background using a wash? • Can they use a range of brushes to create different effects?	• Do they sing in tune with expression? • Do they control their voice when singing? • Can they play clear notes on instruments?

The Learning Challenge™
CURRICULUM

Year 3: Do you think that Sir Titus Salt was a hero or a villain?

KS2 History: Local History - A study of Local History taking account of a period of history that shaped the locality

WOW: Children to consider all the places and buildings that are associated with Sir Titus Salt, eg, Salt Park.

LC1	Who was Sir Titus Salt and why is he important to the people of Bradford?
LC2	What was The Industrial Revolution and how did it impact on Bradford?
LC3	Why is Saltaire situated where it is?
LC4	Why is wool important to Bradford?
LC5	How can you use art to capture Bradford at this time?
LC6	Why were young children employed in the mills?
LC7	What would the music of the time have been like?
LC8	Reflection: Set up a courtroom simulation to decide whether Sir Titus Salt was innocent or guilty.

Literacy Link: Opportunities for children to carry out research exist in LC1, LC2, LC3, LC4, LC6 and LC7.

Creative Art Link: In LC5 children will use old photographs and create their own images of Bradford based on LS Lowry's style.

Expressive Art Links: LC7 - Children will perform the music that children would have sung in Victorian times

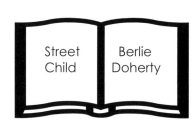

Street Child — Berlie Doherty

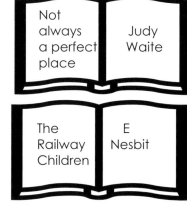

Not always a perfect place — Judy Waite

The Railway Children — E Nesbit

Year 3 History Knowledge, Skills and Understanding breakdown

Chronological understanding	Knowledge and interpretation	Historical enquiry
• Can they describe events from the past using dates when things happened? • Can they use a timeline within a specific period in history to set out the order events may have happened? • Can they use their mathematical knowledge to work out how long ago events would have happened?	• Can they suggest why certain events happened as they did in history? • Can they suggest why certain people acted as they did in history?	• Can they use various sources of evidence to answer questions? • Can they use various sources to piece together information about a period in history? • Can they research a specific event from the past ? • Can they use their 'information finding' skills in writing to help them write about historical information? • Can they, through research, identify similarities and differences between given periods in history?

Year 3 (Challenging)

• Can they set out on a timeline, within a given period, what special events took place?
• Can they begin to use more than one source of information to bring together a conclusion about an historical event?
• Can they use specific search engines on the Internet to help them find information more rapidly?

Knowledge, Skills and Understanding breakdown for Art and Music

Art & Design	Music
• Can they use their sketches to produce a final piece of work? • Can they write an explanation of their sketch in notes? • Can they use different grades of pencil shade, to show different tones and texture? • Can they predict with accuracy the colours that they mix? • Do they know where each of the primary and secondary colours sits on the colour wheel? • Can they create a background using a wash? • Can they use a range of brushes to create different effects?	• Do they sing in tune with expression? • Do they control their voice when singing? • Can they play clear notes on instruments?

The Learning Challenge™
CURRICULUM

EDUCATION

Geography and History Learning Challenges

Year 4

The examples that follow are exactly that, examples.

Consider your context without losing sight of National Curriculum coverage when making adaptations to suit your school and pupils' needs.

Geography and History: Year 4 Overview

Key Features					
	GEOGRAPHY		**HISTORY**		
	Human	Physical	The Roman Empire and its impact on Britain	A Study of an aspect or theme in British history, beyond 1066	A Study of an aspect or theme in British history, beyond 1066
Year 4	**River Study and City locations** • Settlements, land use, economic activity, including natural resources, especially water supplies	**UK City Study** • Use maps, atlases, globes and digital/ computer mapping to locate countries and describe features studied	• Julius Caesar • Hadrian's Wall • Boudica • Romanisation of Britain	• Crime and punishment • Leisure and entertainment in the 20th century	• Norman culture • Establishment of feudal system
Possible Learning Challenges	Where would you choose to build a city? or *Why is the Thames/ Mersey so important to London/ Liverpool?*	Why is <city> such a cool place to live?	Why were the Romans so powerful and what did we learn from them?	Who were the early lawmakers? or What would you have done after school 100 years ago?	Why were the Norman castles certainly not bouncy?

Geographical and Historical Knowledge, Skills and Understanding requirements for the National Curriculum

KSU Breakdown – Year 4
Geography and History

Knowledge, Skills and Understanding breakdown for History

Year 4

Chronological understanding	Knowledge and interpretation	Historical enquiry
• Can they plot recent history on a timeline using centuries? • Can they place periods of history on a timeline showing periods of time? • Can they use their mathematical skills to round up time differences into centuries and decades?	• Can they explain how events from the past have helped shape our lives? • Do they appreciate that wars have happened from a very long time ago and are often associated with invasion, conquering or religious differences? • Do they know that people who lived in the past cooked and travelled differently and used different weapons from ours? • Do they recognise that the lives of wealthy people were very different from those of poor people? • Do they appreciate how items found belonging to the past are helping us to build up an accurate picture of how people lived in the past?	• Can they research two versions of an event and say how they differ? • Can they research what it was like for a child in a given period from the past and use photographs and illustrations to present their findings? • Can they give more than one reason to support an historical argument? • Can they communicate knowledge and understanding orally and in writing and offer points of view based upon what they have found out?

Year 4 (Challenging)

• Can they use their mathematical skills to help them work out the time differences between certain major events in history? • Can they begin to build up a picture of what main events happened in Britain/ the world during different centuries?	• Can they recognise that people's way of life in the past was dictated by the work they did? • Do they appreciate that the food people ate was different because of the availability of different sources of food? • Do they appreciate that weapons will have changed by the developments and inventions that would have occurred within a given time period? • Do they appreciate that wealthy people would have had a very different way of living which would have impacted upon their health and education?	• Can they independently, or as part of a group, present an aspect they have researched about a given period of history using multi-media skills when doing so?

Knowledge, Skills and Understanding breakdown for Geography

Year 4

Geographical Enquiry	Physical Geography	Human Geography	Geographical Knowledge
• Can they carry out a survey to discover features of cities and villages? • Can they find the same place on a globe and in an atlas? • Can they label the same features on an aerial photograph as on a map? • Can they plan a journey to a place in England? • Can they accurately measure and collect information(e.g. rainfall, temperature, wind speed, noise levels etc.)?	• Can they describe the main features of a well-known city? • Can they describe the main features of a village? • Can they describe the main physical differences between cities and villages? • Can they use appropriate symbols to represent different physical features on a map?	• Can they explain why people are attracted to live in cities? • Can they explain why people may choose to live in a village rather than a city? • Can they explain how a locality has changed over time with reference to human features? • Can they find different views about an environmental issue? What is their view? • Can they suggest different ways that a locality could be changed and improved?	• Can they locate the Tropic of Cancer and the Tropic of Capricorn? • Do they know the difference between the British Isles, Great Britain and UK? • Do they know the countries that make up the European Union? • Can they name up to six cities in the UK and locate them on a map? • Can they locate and name some of the main islands that surround the UK? • Can they name the areas of origin of the main ethnic groups in the UK & in their school?

Year 4 (Challenging)

Geographical Enquiry	Physical Geography	Human Geography	Geographical Knowledge
• Can they give accurate measurements between 2 given places within the UK?	• Can they explain how a locality has changed over time with reference to physical features?	• Can they explain how people are trying to manage their environment?	• Can they name the counties that make up the home counties of London? • Can they name some of the main towns and cities in Yorkshire and Lancashire?

Year 4: Where would you choose to build a city?

KS2 Geography: Settlements, land use, economic activity, including natural resources, especially energy and water supplies

WOW: *Watch a film about the building of skyscrapers in New York or Dubai and discuss why buildings need to be tall in a city.*

LC1	What are the common features you notice when locating all of Europe's/Britain's biggest cities?
LC2	Why do you think rivers were important to the location of major cities?
LC3	Can you choose a major European city and create a brochure to encourage someone to visit?
LC4	Why is the transport system very important in major cities?
LC5	Using paper, how can you create a skyscraper that is at least 2 metres high?
LC6	Can you locate many of the important features on a map of a city?
LC7	What are the major differences between a major city and a small town or village?
LC8	Reflection: Children will use photographs from the internet and become a tourist guide in a well known European country.

Literacy Link: LC1 provides opportunities for children to research some of Europe's famous cities and the relationship they have with rivers. LC3 requires children to use the internet to find out about a European city.

Numeracy Link: LC2: There could be opportunities taken to find out about the length of many of Europe's rivers and then create data packages, etc.
LC4: Looking at how the London underground works could provide some interesting work around geometry.

Creative Art Link: LC5 is designed to get children to design and make a tall building so that they appreciate the issues surrounding building some of the skyscrapers in our cities.

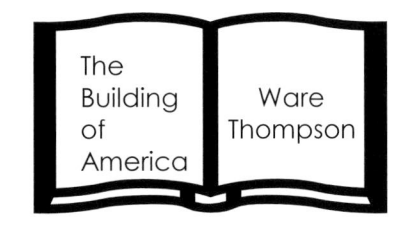

The Building of America

Ware Thompson

Year 4 Geography Knowledge, Skills and Understanding

Geographical Enquiry	Physical Geography	Human Geography	Geographical Knowledge
• Can they carry out a survey to discover features of cities and villages? • Can they find the same place on a globe and in an atlas? • Can they label the same features on an aerial photograph as on a map? • Can they accurately measure and collect information(e.g. rainfall, temperature, wind speed, noise levels etc.)?	• Can they describe the main features of a well-known city? • Can they describe the main features of a village? • Can they describe the main physical differences between cities and villages? • Can they use appropriate symbols to represent different physical features on a map?	• Can they explain why people are attracted to live in cities? • Can they explain why people may choose to live in a village rather than a city? • Can they explain how a locality has changed over time with reference to human features? • Can they find different views about an environmental issue? What is their view?	• Do they know the difference between the British Isles, Great Britain and UK? • Do they know the countries that make up the European Union? • Can they name up to six cities in the UK and locate them on a map? • Can they name the areas of origin of the main ethnic groups in the UK & in their school?

Year 4 (Challenging)

• Can they give accurate measurements between 2 given places within the UK?
• Can they explain how a locality has changed over time with reference to physical features?
• Can they explain how people are trying to manage their environment?

The Learning Challenge™
CURRICULUM

© Focus Education 2014

Year 4 Design Technology Knowledge, Skills and Understanding

Developing, planning and communicating ideas	Working with tools, equipment, materials and components to make quality products	Evaluating processes and products
• Can they come up with at least one idea about how to create their product? • Do they take account of the ideas of others when designing? • Can they produce a plan and explain it to others? • Can they suggest some improvements and say what was good and not so good about their original design?	• Can they tell if their finished product is going to be good quality? • Are they conscious of the need to produce something that will be liked by others? • Can they show a good level of expertise when using a range of tools and equipment?	• Have they thought of how they will check if their design is successful? • Can they begin to explain how they can improve their original design? • Can they evaluate their product, thinking of both its appearance and the way it works?

Breadth of study

Stiff and flexible sheet materials
• Can they measure carefully so as to make sure they have not made mistakes?
• How have they attempted to make their product strong?

Mouldable materials
• Do they take time to consider how they could have made their idea better?
• Do they work at their product even though their original idea might not have worked?

Year 4: Why is the *Thames* so important to *London*?

**Alternative to 'Where would you choose to build a city?'

KS2 Geography: Settlements, land use, economic activity, including natural resources, especially energy and water supplies

WOW: Ideally a boat trip down the Thames

LC1	Why is London situated where it is?
LC2	Which other famous European cities are situated on a river?
LC3	Why are rivers important for the lives of the people who live there now and lived there some time ago?
LC4	How have people adapted rivers and water for their own use?
LC5	How has the Thames created jobs for many people who live in London?
LC6	Using your photographs, can you create a painting of one of the bridges on the Thames?
LC7	Which pieces of music are associated with London or water?
LC8	Reflection: Groups of children to put together a photostory of their learning about London

Literacy Link: LC1 and LC2 provide opportunities for children to carry out their own research

History Link: Opportunities for research into London over the past 100 year or so. This would involve looking at old maps, etc.

Creative Art Link: LC6 provides opportunities for children to look at the work of famous artists and to use water colour or washes to create landscape paintings to include the River Thames.

Expressive Art Link: LC7 provides opportunities for children to think of/ perform the music associated with London or with water.

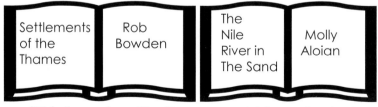

Settlements of the Thames	Rob Bowden	The Nile River in The Sand	Molly Aloian

*This Learning Challenge could be adapted to the River Mersey or Tyne or any other major UK river and city.

Year 4 Geography Knowledge, Skills and Understanding

Geographical Enquiry	Physical Geography	Human Geography	Geographical Knowledge
• Can they carry out a survey to discover features of cities and villages? • Can they find the same place on a globe and in an atlas? • Can they label the same features on an aerial photograph as on a map? • Can they plan a journey to a place in England? • Can they accurately measure and collect information(e.g. rainfall, temperature, wind speed, noise levels etc.)?	• Can they describe the main features of a well-known city? • Can they describe the main features of a village? • Can they describe the main physical differences between cities and villages? • Can they use appropriate symbols to represent different physical features on a map?	• Can they explain why people are attracted to live in cities? • Can they explain why people may choose to live in a village rather than a city? • Can they explain how a locality has changed over time with reference to human features? • Can they find different views about an environmental issue? What is their view? • Can they suggest different ways that a locality could be changed and improved?	• Do they know the difference between the British Isles, Great Britain and UK? • Can they name up to six cities in the UK and locate them on a map? • Can they name the areas of origin of the main ethnic groups in the UK & in their school?

Year 4 (Challenging)

• Can they give accurate measurements between 2 given places within the UK?	• Can they explain how a locality has changed over time with reference to physical features?	• Can they explain how people are trying to manage their environment?	• Can they name the counties that make up the home counties of London?

Year 4 Art & Design Knowledge, Skills and Understanding

Drawing	Painting	Knowledge	Sketch books
• Can they organise line, tone, shape and colour to represent figures and forms in movement? • Can they show reflections? • Can they explain why they have chosen specific materials to draw with?	• Can they create all the colours they need? • Can they create mood in their paintings? • Do they successfully use shading to create mood and feeling?	• Can they experiment with different styles which artists have used? • Can they explain art from other periods of history?	• Can they use their sketch books to express their feelings about various subjects and outline likes and dislikes? • Do they use their sketch books to adapt and improve their original ideas? • Do they keep notes about the purpose of their work in their sketch books?

Year 4 Music Knowledge, Skills and Understanding

- Can they explain the place of silence and say what effect it has?
- Can they start to identify the character of a piece of music?
- Can they describe and identify the different purposes of music?
- Can they begin to identify with the style of work of Beethoven, Mozart and Elgar?
- Can they perform a simple part rhythmically?
- Can they sing songs from memory with accurate pitch?
- Can they improvise using repeated patterns?

The Learning Challenge™
CURRICULUM

Year 4: Why is *London such a cool place to live?

KS2 Geography: name and locate counties and cities of the United Kingdom, geographical regions and their identifying human and physical characteristics, including hills, mountains, cities, rivers, key topographical features and land-use patterns; and understand how some of these aspects have changed over time.

WOW: *Visit to the city chosen – preferably open bus top.*

LC1	Why do you think London is the capital city of the United Kingdom?
LC2	Why do so many people live in London?
LC3	Can you trace the growth in London's population over the past 100 years?
LC4	Can you chose 5 popular monuments or buildings in London and write a promotion leaflet on them?
LC5	Can you reconstruct a bridge that opens to allow a ship to pass?
LC6	From photographs you have taken can you paint one of your favourite places in London?
LC7	What would be the main advantages and disadvantages of living in London?
LC8	Reflection: Using photographs and video extracts can they put together a documentary about the city?

Literacy Link : Huge opportunities in LC4 for children to put together a persuasive style piece of writing linked to the brochures.
In addition, a summary style piece of writing is Required for LC7.

Numeracy Link : LC1 provides opportunities for children to carry out surveys about why people like or dislike the city.
LC3 also provides opportunities for children to look at the figures associated with London's growing population.

Creative Art Link: LC5 provides opportunities for children to design and make a bridge that has a level attached so that it can open.

Creative Art Link: LC6 provides opportunities for children to create their own water colours or washes linked to their paintings.

*Use the nearest major city to you, e.g. Manchester, Birmingham, Newcastle, Bristol, Cardiff or Liverpool.

The Learning Challenge™
CURRICULUM

Year 4 Geography Knowledge, Skills and Understanding

Geographical Enquiry	Physical Geography	Human Geography	Geographical Knowledge
• Can they carry out a survey to discover features of cities and villages? • Can they find the same place on a globe and in an atlas? • Can they label the same features on an aerial photograph as on a map? • Can they accurately measure and collect information(e.g. rainfall, temperature, wind speed, noise levels etc.)?	• Can they describe the main features of a well-known city? • Can they describe the main features of a village? • Can they describe the main physical differences between cities and villages? • Can they use appropriate symbols to represent different physical features on a map?	• Can they explain why people are attracted to live in cities? • Can they explain why people may choose to live in a village rather than a city? • Can they explain how a locality has changed over time with reference to human features? • Can they find different views about an environmental issue? What is their view? • Can they suggest different ways that a locality could be changed and improved?	• Do they know the difference between the British Isles, Great Britain and UK? • Can they name up to six cities in the UK and locate them on a map? • Can they name the areas of origin of the main ethnic groups in the UK & in their school?
Year 4 (Challenging)			
• Can they give accurate measurements between 2 given places within the UK?	• Can they explain how a locality has changed over time with reference to physical features?	• Can they explain how people are trying to manage their environment?	• Can they name the counties that make up the home counties of London?

The Learning Challenge™
CURRICULUM

Year 4 Design Technology Knowledge, Skills and Understanding

Developing, planning and communicating ideas	Working with tools, equipment, materials and components to make quality products	Evaluating processes and products
• Can they come up with at least one idea about how to create their product? • Do they take account of the ideas of others when designing? • Can they produce a plan and explain it to others? • Can they suggest some improvements and say what was good and not so good about their original design?	• Can they tell if their finished product is going to be good quality? • Are they conscience of the need to produce something that will be liked by others? • Can they show a good level of expertise when using a range of tools and equipment?	• Have they thought of how they will check if their design is successful? • Can they begin to explain how they can improve their original design? • Can they evaluate their product, thinking of both its appearance and the way it works?
Electrical and mechanical components • Can they add things to their circuits?	**Stiff and flexible sheet materials** • Can they measure carefully so as to make sure they have not made mistakes? • How have they attempted to make their product strong?	**Mouldable materials** • Do they take time to consider how they could have made their idea better? • Do they work at their product even though their original idea might not have worked?

Year 4 Art & Design Knowledge, Skills and Understanding

Drawing	Painting	Knowledge	Sketch Books
• Can they organise line, tone, shape and colour to represent figures and forms in movement? • Can they show reflections? • Can they explain why they have chosen specific materials to draw with?	• Can they create all the colours they need? • Can they create mood in their paintings? • Do they successfully use shading to create mood and feeling?	• Can they experiment with different styles which artists have used? • Can they explain art from other periods of history?	• Can they use their sketch books to express their feelings about various subjects and outline likes and dislikes? • Do they use their sketch books to adapt and improve their original ideas? • Do they keep notes about the purpose of their work in their sketch books?

The Learning Challenge™
CURRICULUM

Year 4: Why were the Romans so powerful and what did we learn from them?

KS2 History: The Roman Empire and its impact on Britain
- Julius Caesar
- Hadrian's Wall
- Boudica
- Romanisation of Britain

WOW: *Class to be given surprise 'extra' playtime so that an older group of children can 'invade' their classroom.*

LC1	What is it like to be invaded and which countries have been invaded recently?
LC2	Who were the Romans and would they have enjoyed coming to Britain?
LC3	Would you prefer to be a Gladiator or a Premiership footballer?
LC4	What did the Romans do for us?
LC5	How could you be as fit as a Roman?
LC6	Why did the Romans need to build forts?
LC7	Who was Boudica and why did she become so famous?
LC7	Can you create a working model of a Roman weapon?
LC8	Who were the famous Romans and what do we know about them?
LC9	Reflection: Children through 'home learning' tasks will be expected to put together a 'research file' that will start with a range of questions they will have thought of.

Literacy Link: LC1 provides ample opportunities for children to express themselves after being 'invaded' by another class.
LC2 provides research opportunities based on finding out about the Romans.
LC3 offers further research opportunities through finding out about the lives of Gladiators.
LC8 will give children a chance to carry out their own research on one famous Roman. They will then have to do a presentation to the class about their chosen Roman.

Expressive Art Link: During LC5 children will experience marching carrying the equivalent of the Roman's armour.

Creative Arts Link: LC7 will provide children with a chance to research and then design and make a Roman weapon that would have been used to help them capture cities, etc.

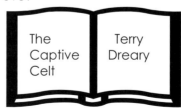

The Captive Celt — Terry Dreary

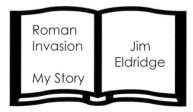

Roman Invasion — My Story — Jim Eldridge

Year 4 History Knowledge, Skills and Understanding breakdown

Chronological understanding	Knowledge and interpretation	Historical enquiry
• Can they plot recent history on a timeline using centuries? • Can they place periods of history on a timeline showing periods of time? • Can they use their mathematical skills to round up time differences into centuries and decades?	• Can they explain how events from the past have helped shape our lives? • Do they appreciate that wars have happened from a very long time ago and are often associated with invasion, conquering or religious differences? • Do they know that people who lived in the past cooked and travelled differently and used different weapons from ours? • Do they recognise that the lives of wealthy people were very different from those of poor people? • Do they appreciate how items found belonging to the past are helping us to build up an accurate picture of how people lived in the past?	• Can they research two versions of an event and say how they differ? • Can they research what it was like for a child in a given period from the past and use photographs and illustrations to present their findings? • Can they give more than one reason to support an historical argument? • Can they communicate knowledge and understanding orally and in writing and offer points of view based upon what they have found out?

Year 4 (Challenging)

• Can they use their mathematical skills to help them work out the time differences between certain major events in history? • Can they begin to build up a picture of what main events happened in Britain/ the world during different centuries?	• Do they appreciate that the food people ate was different because of the availability of different sources of food? • Do they appreciate that weapons will have changed by the developments and inventions that would have occurred within a given time period? • Do they appreciate that wealthy people would have had a very different way of living which would have impacted upon their health and education?	• Can they independently, or as part of a group, present an aspect they have researched about a given period of history using multi-media skills when doing so?

The Learning Challenge™
CURRICULUM

Year 4 Design Technology Knowledge, Sills and Understanding			
Developing, planning and communicating ideas	**Working with tools, equipment, materials and components to make quality products**	**Evaluating processes and products**	**Stiff and Flexible Materials**
• Can they come up with at least one idea about how to create their product? • Do they take account of the ideas of others when designing? • Can they produce a plan and explain it to others? • Can they suggest some improvements and say what was good and not so good about their original design?	• Can they tell if their finished product is going to be good quality? • Are they conscious of the need to produce something that will be liked by others? • Can they show a good level of expertise when using a range of tools and equipment?	• Have they thought of how they will check if their design is successful? • Can they begin to explain how they can improve their original design? • Can they evaluate their product, thinking of both its appearance and the way it works?	• Can they measure carefully so as to make sure they have not made mistakes? • How have they attempted to make their product strong?

Year 4: Who were the early lawmakers?

KS2 History: crime and punishment from the Anglo Saxons to the present day

WOW: *Work together to create rules to make their class the most important in the whole school (Bias).*
Visit from a community police-officer.

LC1	Why do we need laws and who thought of them in the first place?
LC2	What is the Magna Carta and why is it so important even today?
LC3	What is a Parliament and what is its connection to laws?
LC4	Who created the first British Parliament and how did it work?
LC5	Who makes our laws today and who upholds them?
LC6	What were punishments like 750 years ago?
LC7	Reflection: Recreate a court held in the 12th or 13th century.

Literacy Link: Huge opportunities in LC1 for children to list the laws they would like to have and the ones they would do away with. This can be linked to rules in school.
LC2 provides research opportunities for children to find out about the way our country's laws were made.
LC4 provides children with a chance to find out more about de Montfort's parliament and how it differed to what we know today.
LC6 provides children with good opportunities to have fun with what would now be strange punishments.

Numeracy Link: There continues to be good opportunities for children to think about dates and 'how long ago' as they look at how laws have changed.

Creative Link: During LC3 children should be encouraged to draw the Houses of Parliament giving good attention to line, tone, and perspective.

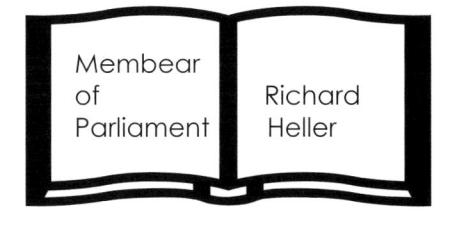

Membear of Parliament   Richard Heller

Year 4 History Knowledge, Skills and Understanding

Chronological understanding	Knowledge and interpretation	Historical enquiry
• Can they describe events and periods using the words: BC, AD and decade? • Can they plot recent history on a timeline using centuries? • Can they place periods of history on a timeline showing periods of time? • Can they use their mathematical skills to round up time differences into centuries and decades?	• Can they explain how events from the past have helped shape our lives? • Can they recognise how lives in the past are different from ours? • Do they know that people who lived in the past cooked and travelled differently and used different weapons from ours? • Do they recognise that the lives of wealthy people were very different from those of poor people? • Do they appreciate how items found belonging to the past are helping us to build up an accurate picture of how people lived in the past?	• Can they research two versions of an event and say how they differ? • Can they give more than one reason to support an historical argument? • Can they communicate knowledge and understanding orally and in writing and offer points of view based upon what they have found out? • Do they appreciate how historical artefacts like the Magna Carta have helped us understand more about British lives in the present and past?

Year 4 (Challenging)

• Can they use their mathematical skills to help them work out the time differences between certain major events in history? • Can they begin to build up a picture of what main events happened in Britain/ the world during different centuries?	• Can they recognise that people's way of life in the past was dictated by the work they did? • Do they appreciate that wealthy people would have had a very different way of living which would have impacted upon their health and education?	• Can they independently, or as part of a group, present an aspect they have researched about a given period of history using multi-media skills when doing so?

The Learning Challenge™
CURRICULUM

Year 4 Art & Design Knowledge, Skills and Understanding

Drawing	Painting	Knowledge	Sketch books
• Can they identify and draw simple objects, and use marks and lines to produce texture? • Can they organise line, tone, shape and colour to represent figures and forms in movement? • Can they show reflections? • Can they explain why they have chosen specific materials to draw with?	• Can they create all the colours they need? • Can they create mood in their paintings? • Do they successfully use shading to create mood and feeling?	• Can they experiment with different styles which artists have used? • Can they explain art from other periods of history?	• Can they use their sketch books to express their feelings about various subjects and outline likes and dislikes? • Do they use their sketch books to adapt and improve their original ideas? • Do they keep notes about the purpose of their work in their sketch books?

Year 4: What would you have done after school 100 years ago?

KS2 History: Leisure and Entertainment in the 20th century

WOW: All children start the day by being introduced to traditional board games such as: ludo; snakes and ladders, etc.

LC1	How would you have coped without television and the iPad?
LC2	How was leisure and entertainment different for rich and poor children 100 years ago?
LC3	Would you have been able to go to McDonald's for your birthday party 100 years ago?
LC4	What would your favourite football team have looked like 100 years ago?
LC5	How could you create your own 'Silent Movie'?
LC6	What would 'Top of the Pops' have been like 100 years ago?
LC7	Reflection: Children to create a documentary on life for children 100 years ago focusing on leisure and entertainment

Literacy Link: Huge opportunities in LC1 for children to consider what life would be like without television and electronic gadgets. LC2 provides research opportunities for children to find out about what rich children would have had in comparison to poor ones. LC3 provides children with a chance to find out about how children would have celebrated birthdays and Christmas. LC4 provides children with good opportunities to research what footballers would have worn and then to find out about how much it would have cost to watch them play, etc. Use old football, programmes to find out more about life from the adverts, etc.

IT Presentation: During LC5 children will have to write and produce their own silent movie and film it. Further opportunities for IT presentation offered in LC6

Expressive Link: During LC6 children will find out about the popular songs of the era and then create their own video dressed appropriately for the time.

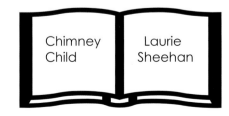

Chimney Child   Laurie Sheehan

Year 4 History Knowledge, Skills and Understanding

Chronological understanding	Knowledge and interpretation	Historical enquiry
• Can they plot recent history on a timeline using centuries? • Can they place periods of history on a timeline showing periods of time? • Can they use their mathematical skills to round up time differences into centuries and decades?	• Can they explain how events from the past has helped shape our lives? • Can they recognise how lives in the past are different from ours? • Do they know that people who lived in the past cooked and travelled differently and used different weapons from ours? • Do they recognise that the lives of wealthy people were very different from those of poor people? • Do they appreciate how items found belonging to the past are helping us to build up an accurate picture of how people lived in the past?	• Can they research two versions of an event and say how they differ? • Can they give more than one reason to support an historical argument? • Can they communicate knowledge and understanding orally and in writing and offer points of view based upon what they have found out?

Year 4 (Challenging)

• Can they use their mathematical skills to help them work out the time differences between certain major events in history? • Can they begin to build up a picture of what main events happened in Britain/ the world during different centuries?	• Can they recognise that people's way of life in the past was dictated by the work they did? • Do they appreciate that wealthy people would have had a very different way of living which would have impacted upon their health and education?	• Can they independently, or as part of a group, present an aspect they have researched about a given period of history using multi-media skills when doing so?

Year 4 Music Knowledge, Skills and Understanding

• Can they perform a simple part rhythmically?
• Can they sing songs from memory with accurate pitch?
• Can they improvise using repeated patterns?
• Can they start to identify the character of a piece of music?
• Can they describe and identify the different purposes of music?
• Can they begin to identify with the style of work of significant British musicians?

Year 4: Why were the Norman castles certainly not bouncy?

KS2 History. A study of an aspect or theme in British history that extends beyond 1066: The Norman invasion and its impact on British society.

WOW: Invite children to bring in toy castles that they have at home and then discuss what they are used for and how accurate their toys are. Possible visit to local castle.

LC1	Why did the Normans build so many castles?
LC2	Who was William the Conqueror and why is 1066 a famous date in British history?
LC3	How do we know what happened in 1066 and how could we produce a similar 'collage' to explain what happened in Britain this year?
LC4	What do you know about the Motte and Bailey castle and can you design one?
LC5	Using clay can you create a piece of art that captures a Norman castle?
LC6	What is the Domesday Book and do we have something similar today?
LC7	What changed in Britain as a result of the Norman conquest?
LC8	Reflection: In small groups, using small models, can they recreate a battle of a siege of a castle and film it.

Literacy Link: It is important that the research in LC1helps children realise that castles were built to create safe areas for the conquering armies. LC2 provides further research opportunities when they focus on one famous person from our history.

Numeracy Link: Children will need to make use of their measurement skills when designing their Motte and Bailey castle.

Creative Arts: Children to examine the Bayeux Tapestry and try to recreate a collage to capture life today.

Creative Art Link: Children in LC3 will have to carry out research on Motte and Bailey castles before designing and making one.

Creative Art Link: In LC5 children will work on a clay plaque which depicts a Norman castle theme.

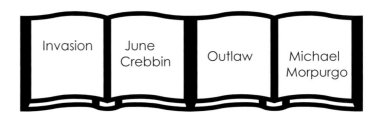

Invasion | June Crebbin | Outlaw | Michael Morpurgo

The Learning Challenge™ CURRICULUM

Year 4 History Knowledge, Skills and Understanding

Chronological understanding	Knowledge and interpretation	Historical enquiry
• Can they describe events and periods using the words: BC, AD and decade? • Can they plot recent history on a timeline using centuries? • Can they place periods of history on a timeline showing periods of time? • Can they use their mathematical skills to round up time differences into centuries and decades?	• Can they explain how events from the past have helped shape our lives? • Can they recognise how lives in the past are different from ours? • Do they know that people who lived in the past cooked and travelled differently and used different weapons from ours? • Do they recognise that the lives of wealthy people were very different from those of poor people? • Do they appreciate how items found belonging to the past are helping us to build up an accurate picture of how people lived in the past?	• Can they research two versions of an event and say how they differ? • Can they research what it was like for a child in a given period from the past and use photographs and illustrations to present their findings? • Can they give more than one reason to support an historical argument? • Can they communicate knowledge and understanding orally and in writing and offer points of view based upon what they have found out? • Do they appreciate how historical artefacts like the Domesday Book have helped us understand more about British lives in the present and past?

Year 4 (Challenging)

• Can they use their mathematical skills to help them work out the time differences between certain major events in history? • Can they begin to build up a picture of what main events happened in Britain/ the world during different centuries?	• Do they appreciate that weapons will have changed by the developments and inventions that would have occurred within a given time period? • Do they appreciate that wealthy people would have had a very different way of living which would have impacted upon their health and education?	• Can they independently, or as part of a group, present an aspect they have researched about a given period of history using multi-media skills when doing so?

The Learning Challenge™
CURRICULUM

Year 4 Design Technology Knowledge, Skills and Understanding

Developing, planning and communicating ideas	Working with tools, equipment, materials and components to make quality products	Evaluating processes and products
• Do they take account of the ideas of others when designing? • Can they produce a plan and explain it to others? • Can they suggest some improvements and say what was good and not so good about their original design?	• Can they tell if their finished product is going to be good quality? • Are they conscious of the need to produce something that will be liked by others? • Can they show a good level of expertise when using a range of tools and equipment?	• Have they thought of how they will check if their design is successful? • Can they begin to explain how they can improve their original design? • Can they evaluate their product, thinking of both its appearance and the way it works?

Breadth of study

Stiff and flexible sheet materials
• Can they measure carefully so as to make sure they have not made mistakes?
• How have they attempted to make their product strong?

Mouldable materials
• Do they take time to consider how they could have made their idea better?
• Do they work at their product even though their original idea might not have worked?

Year 4 Art & Design Knowledge, Skills and Understanding

• Can they identify and draw simple objects, and use marks and lines to produce texture?
• Can they begin to sculpt clay and other mouldable materials?
• Can they explain art from other periods of history?

The Learning Challenge™
CURRICULUM

Geography and History Learning Challenges

Year 5

The examples that follow are exactly that, examples.

Consider your context without losing sight of National Curriculum coverage when making adaptations to suit your school and pupils' needs.

Geography and History: Year 5 Overview

	Key Features				
	GEOGRAPHY		**HISTORY**		
	Human	**Physical**	Anglo Saxons, • Settlements and kingdoms • Art and Culture • Christianity conversion	Early Civilizations • Ancient Egyptians • Ancient Sumer • Indus Valley • Shang Dynasty of Ancient China	A Study of an aspect or theme in British history, beyond 1066 • The execution of Charles 1 • Hitler's invasion of Poland and its impact on Britain
Year 5	**Brazil** • Trade and growing economy • Fair Trade	Rainforests of the Amazon **Brazil** – physical features			
	• locate the world's countries, using maps to focus on Europe and North and South America and concentrating on their environmental regions, key physical and human characteristics, countries, and major cities				
Possible Learning Challenges	**Why is Brazil in the news again? or What's so special about the USA?**	**Why should the rainforests be important to us all?**	**Were the Anglo-Saxons really smashing?**	**How can we re-discover the wonder of Ancient Egypt?**	**Why should gunpowder, treason and plot never be forgotten? Or How could Hitler have convinced a nation like Germany to have followed him?**

The Learning Challenge™
CURRICULUM

Geographical and Historical Knowledge, Skills and Understanding requirements for the National Curriculum

KSU Breakdown – Year 5
Geography and History

Knowledge, Skills and Understanding breakdown for History

Year 5

Chronological understanding	Knowledge and interpretation	Historical enquiry
• Can they use dates and historical language in their work? • Can they draw a timeline with different time periods outlined which show different information, such as, periods of history, when famous people lived, etc.? • Can they use their mathematical skills to work out exact time scales and differences as need be?	• Can they describe historical events from the different period/s they are studying/have studied? • Can they make comparisons between historical periods; explaining things that have changed and things which have stayed the same? • Can they explain the role that Britain has had in spreading Christian values across the world? • Can they begin to appreciate that how we make decisions has been through a Parliament for some time? • Do they appreciate that significant events in history have helped shape the country we have today? • Do they have a good understanding as to how crime and punishment has changed over the years?	• Can they test out a hypothesis in order to answer a question? • Do they appreciate how historical artefacts have helped us understand more about British lives in the present and past?

Year 5 (Challenging)

• Can they create timelines which outline the development of specific features, such as medicine; weaponry; transport, etc.	• Do they appreciate how plagues and other major events have created huge differences to the way medicines and health care was developed?	• Can they research the life of one person who has had an influence on the way Great Britain is divided into four separate countries?

Knowledge, Skills and Understanding breakdown for Geography

Year 5

Geographical Enquiry	Physical Geography	Human Geography	Geographical Knowledge
• Can they collect information about a place and use it in a report? • Can they map land use? • Can they find possible answers to their own geographical questions? • Can they make detailed sketches and plans; improving their accuracy later? • Can they plan a journey to a place in another part of the world, taking account of distance and time?	• Can they explain why many cities of the world are situated by rivers? • Can they explain how a location fits into its wider geographical location; with reference to physical features? • Can they explain how the water cycle works? • Can they explain why water is such a valuable commodity?	• Can they explain why people are attracted to live by rivers? • Can they explain how a location fits into its wider geographical location; with reference to human and economical features? • Can they explain what a place might be like in the future, taking account of issues impacting on human features?	• Can they name and locate many of the world's major rivers on maps? • Can they name and locate many of the world's most famous mountain regions on maps? • Can they locate the USA and Canada on a world map and atlas? • Can they locate and name the main countries in South America on a world map and atlas?

Year 5 (Challenging)

Geographical Enquiry	Physical Geography	Human Geography	Geographical Knowledge
• Can they work out an accurate itinerary detailing a journey to another part of the world?	• Can they explain what a place (open to environmental and physical change) might be like in the future taking account of physical features?	• Can they report on ways in which humans have both improved and damaged the environment?	• Can they begin to recognise the climate of a given country according to its location on the map?

Year 5: Why is Brazil in the news again?

KS2 Geography: locate the world's countries, using maps, to focus on South America and concentrating on their key physical and human characteristics, countries, and major cities.

WOW: *Show a special video about Brazil which captures the main aspects of the country*

LC1	What do you already know about Brazil?
LC2	What fruits and other natural resources is Brazil famous for?
LC3	Which famous cities in Brazil attract tourists and why?
LC4	What can you find out about one of Brazil's neighbouring countries?
LC5	Can you design and create a collage of Brazilian symbols?
LC6	Why is Brazil famous for its dancing?
LC7	What can you find out about the street children of Brazil?
LC8	What can you find out about a famous Brazilian?
LC9	Reflection: The children to host a Brazil day for their parents.

Literacy Link: There are many opportunities for children to carry out research in LC2, LC4, LC7 and LC8.
In LC4 children will choose different countries and do a presentation to the others in their class.
For LC3 children will create a brochure on a Brazilian city.

Creative Art Link: In LC5 children will research the many symbols associated with Brazil and use the symbols to create a montage of Brazil.

Expressive Art Link: In LC6 children will find out about samba dancing and then perform some Brazilian style dancing.

Running Wild   Michael Morpurgo

The Learning Challenge™ CURRICULUM

Year 5 Geography Knowledge, Skills and Understanding

Geographical Enquiry	Physical Geography	Human Geography	Geographical Knowledge
• Can they collect information about a place and use it in a report? • Can they find possible answers to their own geographical questions? • Can they plan a journey to a place in another part of the world, taking account of distance and time?	• Can they explain why many cities of the world are situated by rivers? • Can they explain how a location fits into its wider geographical location; with reference to physical features?	• Can they explain why people are attracted to live by rivers? • Can they explain how a location fits into its wider geographical location; with reference to human and economical features?	• Can they locate and name the main countries in South America on a world map and atlas?
Year 5 (Challenging)			
• Can they work out an accurate itinerary detailing a journey to another part of the world?	• Can they explain what a place (open to environmental and physical change) might be like in the future taking account of physical features?	• Can they report on ways in which humans have both improved and damaged the environment?	• Can they begin to recognise the climate of a given country according to its location on the map?

Year 5 Art & Design Knowledge, Skills and Understanding

- Can they create a piece of art work which includes the integration of digital images they have taken?
- Can they combine graphics and text based on their research?
- Can they combine visual and tactile qualities?
- Do they learn about the work of others by looking at their work in books, the internet, visits to galleries and other sources of information?
- Do they keep notes in their sketch books as to how they might develop their work further?
- Do they use their sketch books to compare and discuss ideas with others?

Year 5 Dance Knowledge, Skills and Understanding

- Do they plan and perform dances confidently?
- Can they compose motifs and plan dances creatively and collaboratively in groups?
- Can they adapt and refine the way they use weight, space and rhythm in their dances to express themselves in the style of dance they use?
- Can they perform different styles of dance clearly and fluently?
- Do they organise their own warm-up and cool-down exercises?
- Can they recognise and comment on dances, showing an understanding of style?
- Can they suggest ways to improve their own and other people's work?
- Do they use their understanding of composition to create dance phrases for themselves and others in their group?
- Do they use their knowledge of dance to adapt their skills to meet the demands of a range of dance styles?
- Can they show expression in their dances and sensitivity to music?

Year 5: What's so special about the USA?

***Alternative to 'Why is Brazil in the news again?'**

KS2 Geography: locate the world's countries, using maps to focus on North America and concentrating on their key physical and human characteristics, countries, and major cities.

WOW: *Look at a series of photographs of workers building the skyscrapers of New York.*

LC1	What would you ask the President of the USA?
LC2	Why is New York one of the world's most visited cities?
LC3	Can you carry out your own research on one of the American states?
LC4	Using the art of Andy Warhol, can you recreate his work using a famous American as your subject?
LC5	Who were the original Americans?
LC6	What can you find out about the sports Americans play?
LC7	How can you create your own silent movie?
LC8	What do you know about the climate of the USA?
LC9	Reflection: Children to create a documentary which explains why they should visit the USA.

Literacy Link: Children in LC1 have to think of a range of questions they would ask the President if they were to meet him.
LC2 provides children with an opportunity of researching New York from the perspective of: its growth; its position on the Hudson; its importance in world economy, etc.
LC3 provides children with a choice to research a state that they want to find out more about. They will then do a presentation to others of their chosen state.

Creative Art Link: In LC4 children will study the art of Andy Warhol and then use his style to focus on a famous American of their choice.
In LC7 children will have a chance to link with America's fame for films by writing and producing their own silent movie.

Historical Link: In LC5 children can research the history of America and find out who the original Americans were and why there are so many people from different nationalities in the USA.

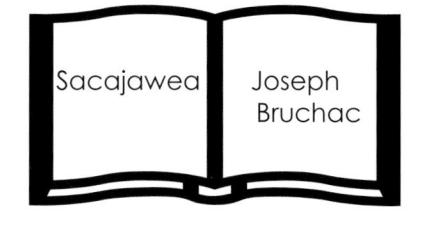

Sacajawea | Joseph Bruchac

Year 5 Geography Knowledge, Skills and Understanding

Geographical Enquiry	Physical Geography	Human Geography	Geographical Knowledge
• Can they collect information about a place and use it in a report? • Can they map land use? • Can they find possible answers to their own geographical questions? • Can they plan a journey to a place in another part of the world, taking account of distance and time?	• Can they explain why many cities of the world are situated by rivers? • Can they explain how a location fits into its wider geographical location; with reference to physical features? • Can they explain why water is such a valuable commodity?	• Can they explain why people are attracted to live by rivers? • Can they explain how a location fits into its wider geographical location; with reference to human and economical features? • Can they explain what a place might be like in the future, taking account of issues impacting on human features?	• Can they name and locate many of the world's major rivers on maps? • Can they name and locate many of the world's most famous mountain regions on maps? • Can they locate the USA and Canada on a world map and atlas?
Year 5 (Challenging)			
• Can they work out an accurate itinerary detailing a journey to another part of the world?	• Can they explain what a place (open to environmental and physical change) might be like in the future taking account of physical features?	• Can they report on ways in which humans have both improved and damaged the environment?	• Can they begin to recognise the climate of a given country according to its location on the map?

The Learning Challenge™
CURRICULUM

Year 5 Art & Design Knowledge, Skills and Understanding

Drawing	Painting	Knowledge	Sketch books
• Do they successfully use shading to create mood and feeling? • Can they organise line, tone, shape and colour to represent figures and forms in movement? • Can they show reflections? • Can they explain why they have chosen specific materials to draw with?	• Can they create all the colours they need? • Can they create mood in their paintings? • Can they express their emotions accurately through their painting and sketches?	• Can they experiment with different styles which artists have used? • Do they learn about the work of others by looking at their work in books, the internet, visits to galleries and other sources of information?	• Do they keep notes in their sketch books as to how they might develop their work further? • Do they use their sketch books to compare and discuss ideas with others?

Year 5 History Knowledge, Skills and Understanding

• Can they use dates and historical language in their work?
• Can they draw a timeline with different time periods outlined which show various information, such as, periods of history, when famous people lived, etc.?
• Can they describe historical events from the different period/s they are studying/have studied?
• Can they make comparisons between historical periods; explaining things that have changed and things which have stayed the same?

Year 5: Why should the rainforest be important to us all?

KS2 Geography: locate the world's countries, using maps to focus on South America and concentrating on their environmental regions, key physical and human characteristics.

WOW: *Show some film clips of the rainforests*

LC1	How can you create your own class rainforest?
LC2	Where are rainforests located and what are their main features?
LC3	Why are rainforests often in the news and what can we do to help?
LC4	What can you find out about an endangered animal that lives in the rainforest?
LC5	How important is the Amazon to the South American rainforests?
LC6	Can you create a print using the large leaves of rainforest plants as your inspiration?
LC7	How would you survive in the rainforest?
LC8	Reflection: Present a documentary on a day in the rainforest

Literacy Link : LC4 provides opportunities for children to carry our their own research and to present their findings in a range of interesting ways which may involve ICT.
LC3 will provide opportunities for children to use their persuasion skills when making cases for saving the rainforests.

Numeracy Link: LC5 provides opportunities for children to use their measurement skills.

Creative Art Link: LC1 sees children working together to design and create their own rainforests. This will involve dividing tasks up between them and making decisions about what they will have within the rainforest.
LC6 sees children using large leaves to create their own design and prints.
LC7 – Design and build shelters

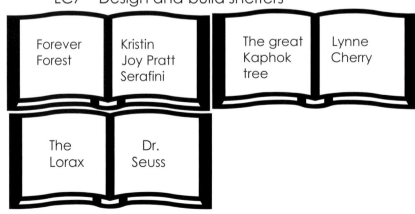

Forever Forest   Kristin Joy Pratt Serafini

The great Kaphok tree   Lynne Cherry

The Lorax   Dr. Seuss

Year 5 Geography Knowledge, Skills and Understanding

Geographical Enquiry	Physical Geography	Human Geography	Geographical Knowledge
• Can they collect information about a place and use it in a report? • Can they find possible answers to their own geographical questions? • Can they make detailed sketches and plans; improving their accuracy later? • Can they plan a journey to a place in another part of the world, taking account of distance and time?	• Can they explain why many cities of the world are situated by rivers? • Can they explain how a location fits into its wider geographical location; with reference to physical features? • Can they explain why water is such a valuable commodity?	• Can they explain why people are attracted to live by rivers? • Can they explain how a location fits into its wider geographical location; with reference to human and economical features? • Can they explain what a place might be like in the future, taking account of issues impacting on human features?	• Can they name and locate many of the world's major rivers on maps? • Can they name and locate many of the world's most famous mountain regions on maps? • Can they locate and name the main countries in South America on a world map and atlas?
Year 5 (Challenging)			
• Can they work out an accurate itinerary detailing a journey to another part of the world?	• Can they explain what a place (open to environmental and physical change) might be like in the future taking account of physical features?	• Can they report on ways in which humans have both improved and damaged the environment?	• Can they begin to recognise the climate of a given country according to its location on the map?

The Learning Challenge™
CURRICULUM

Year 5 Design Technology Knowledge, Skills and Understanding

Developing, planning and communicating ideas

- Can they come up with a range of ideas after they have collected information?
- Do they take a user's view into account when designing?
- Can they produce a detailed step-by-step plan?
- Can they suggest some alternative plans and say what the good points and drawbacks are about each?

Working with tools, equipment, materials and components to make quality products

- Can they explain why their finished product is going to be of good quality?
- Can they explain how their product will appeal to the audience?
- Can they use a range of tools and equipment expertly?

Evaluating processes and products

- Do they keep checking that their design is the best it can be?
- Do they check whether anything could be improved?
- Can they evaluate appearance and function against the original criteria?

Textiles

- Do they think what the user would want when choosing textiles?
- How have they made their product attractive and strong?
- Can they make up a prototype first?
- Can they use a range of joining techniques?

Stiff and flexible sheet materials

- Are their measurements accurate enough to ensure that everything is precise?
- How have they ensured that their product is strong and fit for purpose?

Mouldable materials

- Are they motivated enough to refine and improve their product?
- Do they persevere through different stages of the making process?

Year 5 Art & Design Knowledge, Skills and Understanding

- Can they print using a number of colours?
- Can they create an accurate print design that meets a given criteria?
- Can they print onto different materials?
- Can they create all the colours they need for printing?
- Can they express their emotions accurately through their painting and sketches?
- Do they keep notes in their sketch books as to how they might develop their work further?
- Do they use their sketch books to compare and discuss ideas with others?

The Learning Challenge™
CURRICULUM

Year 5: Were the Anglo-Saxons really smashing?

KS2 History: Britain's settlements by Anglo-Saxons and Scots - Anglo-Saxon invasions; settlements; kingdoms; names and places; art and culture and Christian conversion

WOW: This LC will start with a simulated dig with children having to work out what certain artefacts would have been used for.

LC1	Who were the Anglo-Saxons and how did they influence our life today?
LC2	How did the Anglo-Saxons bring law and order to Britain?
LC3	What evidence do we have today that the Anglo-Saxons were ever here in the first place?
LC4	Which Anglo-Saxon Christian symbols remain with us today?
LC5	Can you create your own Anglo-Saxon art focusing on tessellations?
LC6	Who were the famous Anglo-Saxons and why was Alfred so 'great'?
LC7	Can you work as a group to create a model Anglo-Saxon settlement?
LC8	Reflection: Using your model settlement, can you produce a filmed documentary about Anglo-Saxon life?

Literacy Link: LC1 – Opportunities for research about Anglo-Saxons – focusing on the impact on British history.
LC6 – Opportunities for distinctive research on famous Anglo-Saxons as well as Alfred the Great.
During LC3 children will focus specifically on common names and words we use today that derive from Anglo-Saxon times.

Creative Art Link: During LC5, children will design and make their own jewellery based on the patterns commonly used by Anglo-Saxons.

Creative Art Link: During LC7 children work as a group to design and make an Anglo-Saxon settlement having carried out research in the first instance.

IT Link: During the reflection children will simulate a film of life in an Anglo-Saxon settlement.

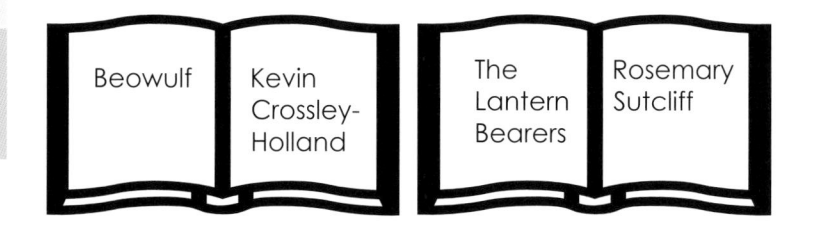

Beowulf | Kevin Crossley-Holland

The Lantern Bearers | Rosemary Sutcliff

The Learning Challenge™
CURRICULUM

Year 5 History Knowledge, Skills and Understanding breakdown

Chronological understanding	Knowledge and interpretation	Historical enquiry
• Can they use dates and historical language in their work? • Can they draw a timeline with different time periods outlined which show a range of information, such as, periods of history, when famous people lived, etc.? • Can they use their mathematical skills to work exact time scales and differences as need be?	• Can they describe historical events from the different period/s they are studying/have studied? • Can they make comparisons between historical periods; explaining things that have changed and things which have stayed the same? • Can they explain the role that Britain has had in spreading Christian values across the world? • Do they appreciate that significant events in history have helped shape the country we have today? • Do they have a good understanding as to how crime and punishment has changes over the years?	• Can they test out a hypothesis in order to answer a question? • Do they appreciate how historical artefacts have helped us understand more about British lives in the present and past?

Year 5 (Challenging)

• Can they create timelines which outline the development of specific features, such as medicine; weaponry; transport, etc.	• Do they appreciate how plagues and other major events have created huge differences to the way medicines and health care was looked at?	• Can they research the life of one person who has had an influence on the way Great Britain is divided into four separate countries?

Year 5 Design Technology Knowledge, Skills and Understanding breakdown for Year 5

• Can they think of some ideas of their own? • Can they explain what they want to do? • Can they use pictures and words to plan?	• Can they explain what they are making? • Can they explain which tools are they using? • Can they describe how something works? • Can they talk about their own work and things that other people have done?	• Can they talk with others about how they want to construct their product? • Can they select appropriate resources and tools for their building projects? • Can they make simple plans before making objects, e.g. drawings, arranging pieces of construction before building?

The Learning Challenge™
CURRICULUM

Year 5: How can we re-discover the wonders of Ancient Egypt?

KS2 History: The achievements of the earliest civilizations – an overview of the impact the Ancient Egyptians had on our society

WOW: *Pupils research 10 facts that they believe to be true about Ancient Egypt*

LC1	Where is Egypt and why do so many people enjoy going on holiday there?
LC2	What is an archaeologist and how have they helped us find out about the past?
LC3	How can you find out how *your town* has changed?
LC4	How can you recreate the wonder of the Pyramids?
LC5	What have we learnt from the Ancient Egyptians writing – (create time capsule)?
LC6	Who were the Pharaohs, and why were they very important?
LC7	What would you ask an Ancient Egyptian?
LC8	How can we all go Strictly Come Egyptian dancing?
LC9	Reflection: Were the Egyptians more advanced than we are?

Literacy Link: LC7 - Children to think of the questions they would wish to ask an Ancient Egyptian, if they met one.
LC1 – Opportunities for research about Egypt – its geographical location and its history.
LC6 – Opportunities for distinctive research on the Pharaohs, about individual pharaohs and how they were regarded.
During LC5 children will discuss what they would leave in a time capsule if they wanted someone to make sense of our way of life in 2000 years time.

IT Link: During LC3 children will take photographs to help them work out what would have been here 50, 100 or even 250 years ago.

Creative Art Link: During LC4, children will design and make their own Pyramids which will contain at least one hidden compartment.

Expressive Art Link: During LC8 children have to find out about Egyptian dances and then perform them as a group.

The Time Travelling Cat	Julia Jarman	The Pharaohs of Ancient Egypt	Elizabeth Payne

Year 5 History Knowledge, Skills and Understanding breakdown

Chronological understanding	Knowledge and interpretation	Historical enquiry
• Can they use dates and historical language in their work? • Can they draw a timeline with different time periods outlined which show a range of information, such as, periods of history? • Can they use their mathematical skills to work exact time scales and differences as need be?	• Can they describe historical events from the different period/s they are studying/have studied? • Can they make comparisons between historical periods; explaining things that have changed and things which have stayed the same? • Do they appreciate that significant events in history have helped shape the country we have today?	• Can they test out a hypothesis in order to answer a question? • Do they appreciate how historical artefacts have helped us understand more about British lives in the present and past?
Year 5 (Challenging)		
• Can they create timelines which outline the development of specific features, such as medicine; weaponry; transport, etc.	• Do they appreciate how plagues and other major events have created huge differences to the way medicines and health care was looked at?	• Can they research the life of one person who has had an influence on the way Great Britain is divided into four separate countries?

© Focus Education 2014

Year 5 Design Technology Knowledge, Skills and Understanding breakdown

Developing, planning and communicating ideas	Working with tools, equipment, materials and components to make quality products	Evaluating processes and products
• Can they come up with a range of ideas after they have collected information? • Do they take a user's view into account when designing? • Can they produce a detailed step-by-step plan? • Can they suggest some alternative plans and say what the good points and drawbacks are about each?	• Can they explain why their finished product is going to be of good quality? • Can they use a range of tools and equipment expertly?	• Do they keep checking that their design is the best it can be? • Do they check whether anything could be improved? • Can they evaluate appearance and function against the original criteria?

Breadth of study

Stiff and flexible sheet materials
• Are their measurements accurate enough to ensure that everything is precise?
• How have they ensured that their product is strong and fit for purpose?

Year 5 Dance Knowledge, Skills and Understanding breakdown

• Do they plan and perform dances confidently?
• Can they compose motifs and plan dances creatively and collaboratively in groups?
• Can they adapt and refine the way they use weight, space and rhythm in their dances to express themselves in the style of dance they use?
• Can they perform different styles of dance clearly and fluently?
• Do they organise their own warm-up and cool-down exercises?
• Do they show an understanding of safe exercising?
• Can they recognise and comment on dances, showing an understanding of style?
• Can they suggest ways to improve their own and other people's work?

The Learning Challenge™
CURRICULUM

Year 5: Why should gunpowder, treason and plot never be forgotten?

KS2 History: A study of an aspect or theme in British history that extends pupils' chronology beyond 1066: The beheading of Charles 1; Civil War; Great Fire of London

WOW: *Consider modern day plots to overthrow governments or monarchies and debate some of the issues.*

LC1	Who were the Roundheads and the Cavaliers?
LC2	Was Oliver Cromwell right to stop the monarchy?
LC3	Why was the execution of Charles 1 a major event in British history?
LC4	Why do you think the monarchy was restored after a short while?
LC5	Why do some people think that the Great Fire was one of the best things that happened to London?
LC6	Can you work with clay tiles to recreate the Great Fire of London?
LC7	Who was Samuel Pepys and would he have been a modern day blogger?
LC8	Reflection: Set up a Parliamentary debate for and against Cromwell, film it and then show parents.

Literacy Links: great opportunities here for children to experience different writing genres.
LC1 - Information finding;
LC2 - Persuasive
LC3 - Research and Explanation
LC4 – Enquiry
In addition LC7 provides great opportunity for children to write their own blogs after considering Pepys' diary.

Creative Art Link: In LC6 children should be encouraged to work together to make tiles of typical London houses and then use clay to capture the raging fire. If completed correctly this should be a major piece of art work to be displayed in school after they have left.

Reflection: Children to film a debate they participate in which considers the pros and cons of Cromwell's commonwealth. They will need to research first and decide which side they will be on.

The Black Madonna — Stella Riley

Year 5 History Knowledge, Skills and Understanding breakdown

Chronological understanding	Knowledge and interpretation	Historical enquiry
• Can they use dates and historical language in their work? • Can they draw a timeline with different time periods outlined which show different information, such as, periods of history, when famous people lived, etc.? • Can they use their mathematical skills to work exact time scales and differences as need be?	• Can they describe historical events from the different period/s they are studying/have studied? • Can they make comparisons between historical periods; explaining things that have changed and things which have stayed the same? • Can they begin to appreciate that how we make decisions has been through a Parliament for some time? • Do they appreciate that significant events in history have helped shape the country we have today? • Do they have a good understanding as to how crime and punishment has changed over the years?	• Can they test out a hypothesis in order to answer a question? • Do they appreciate how historical artefacts have helped us understand more about British lives in the present and past?

Year 5 (Challenging)

• Can they create timelines which outline the development of specific features, such as medicine; weaponry; transport, etc.	• Do they appreciate how plagues and other major events have created huge differences to the way medicines and health care was looked at?	• Can they research the life of one person who has had an influence on our life today?

Year 5 Art & Design Knowledge, Skills and Understanding breakdown

• Can they sculpt clay and other mouldable materials?
• Can they use textile and sewing skills as part of a project, e.g. hanging, textile book, etc.?
• Do they keep notes in their sketch books as to how they might develop their work further?
• Do they use their sketch books to compare and discuss ideas with others?

The Learning Challenge™
CURRICULUM

Year 5: How could Hitler have convinced a nation like Germany to follow him?

KS2 History: A study of an aspect or theme in British history that extends pupils' chronology beyond 1066: Hitler's invasion of Europe and its impact on Britain

WOW: Start with the famous radio broadcast on a Sunday morning that announced to Britain that we were at war with Germany.

LC1	Why did World War 2 start and what part did Hitler have in it?
LC2	Why did the Jewish nation suffer as a result of Hitler coming to power?
LC3	What can we learn about this period from the Anne Frank diaries?
LC4	What happened in Munich in 1938 and why did Britain feel betrayed by Hitler?
LC5	Why was the Battle of Britain significant in World War 2?
LC6	Who was Winston Churchill and what part did he play in the war?
LC7	How have different European artists captured the horror of the war?
LC8	Reflection: Using photographic images sourced from the Internet put together your story as though you lived during this period

Literacy Links: great opportunities here for children to carry out their own research.
LC1 – about Hitler's rise to power;
LC2 – The suffering of the Jews in WW2
LC3 – Anne Frank's Diaries
LC4 – The Munich Treaty
LC5 – The Battle of Britain
LC6 – Winston Churchill

Creative Art Link: In LC7 children should find out about European artists that have captured images of the war and create their own piece of art based on the techniques used by these artists.

Reflection: Children to put together a photostory of their life as though they had lived during this period. They should add appropriate music and a commentary.

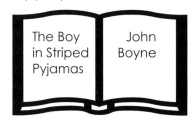

The Boy in Striped Pyjamas — John Boyne

When Hitler Stole Pink Rabbit — Judith Kerr

The Learning Challenge™ CURRICULUM

Year 5 History Knowledge, Skills and Understanding breakdown

Chronological understanding	Knowledge and interpretation	Historical enquiry
• Can they use dates and historical language in their work? • Can they draw a timeline with different time periods outlined which show different information, such as, periods of history, when famous people lived, etc.? • Can they use their mathematical skills to work exact time scales and differences as need be?	• Can they make comparisons between historical periods; explaining things that have changed and things which have stayed the same? • Do they appreciate that significant events in history have helped shape the country we have today? • Do they have a good understanding as to how crime and punishment has changed over the years?	• Can they test out a hypothesis in order to answer a question? • Do they appreciate how historical artefacts have helped us understand more about British lives in the present and past?

Year 5 (Challenging)

• Can they create timelines which outline the development of specific features, such as events in World War 2, etc?	• Do they know the names of the major leaders in Europe and America during World War 2?	• Can they research the life of one person who has had an influence on the way the war ended?

Year 5 Art & Design Knowledge, Skills and Understanding breakdown

- Do they successfully use shading to create mood and feeling?
- Can they organise line, tone, shape and colour to represent figures and forms in movement?
- Can they show reflections?
- Can they explain why they have chosen specific materials to draw with?
- Can they create all the colours they need?
- Can they create mood in their paintings?
- Can they express their emotions accurately through their painting and sketches?
- Do they keep notes in their sketch books as to how they might develop their work further?
- Do they use their sketch books to compare and discuss ideas with others?

The Learning Challenge™
CURRICULUM

Geography and History Learning Challenges

Year 6

The examples that follow are exactly that, examples.

Consider your context without losing sight of National Curriculum coverage when making adaptations to suit your school and pupils' needs.

Geography and History: Year 6 Overview

	Key Features			
	GEOGRAPHY		**HISTORY**	
	Human	**Physical**	**The Vikings and Anglo-Saxon struggles** including:	**A non-European society**
Year 6	The importance of raw materials such as water	Mapping skills and fieldwork	• Viking raids and invasion • Alfred the Great • Viking invasions and Danegeld • Anglo-Saxons law and justice • Edward the Confessor	• Early Islamic civilization • Mayan Civilization • Benin
	• use the eight points of a compass, four-figure grid references, symbols and key (including the use of Ordnance Survey maps) to build their knowledge of the United Kingdom and the wider world • use fieldwork to observe, measure and record the human and physical features in the local area using a range of methods, including sketch maps, plans and graphs, and digital technologies.			
Possible Learning Challenges	I'm a Year 6 pupil, can you get me out of here?	Will you ever see the water you drink again?	Were the Vikings always victorious and vicious?	*Why was the Islamic Civilization around AD900 known as the 'Golden Age'? or *Who were the Mayans and what have we learnt from them ?

Geographical and Historical Knowledge, Skills and Understanding requirements for the National Curriculum

KSU Breakdown – Year 6
Geography and History

Knowledge, Skills and Understanding breakdown for History

Year 6

Chronological understanding	Knowledge and interpretation	Historical enquiry
• Can they say where a period of history fits on a timeline? • Can they place a specific event on a timeline by decade? • Can they place features of historical events and people from past societies and periods in a chronological framework?	• Can they summarise the main events from a specific period in history, explaining the order in which key events happened? • Can they summarise how Britain has had a major influence on world history? • Can they summarise what Britain may have learnt from other countries and civilizations through time gone by and more recently? • Can they describe features of historical events and people from past societies and periods they have studied? • Can they recognise and describe differences and similarities/ changes and continuity between different periods of history?	• Can they look at two different versions and say how the author may be attempting to persuade or give a specific viewpoint? • Can they identify and explain their understanding of propaganda? • Can they describe a key event from Britain's past using a range of evidence from different sources?

Year 6 (Challenging)

Chronological understanding	Knowledge and interpretation	Historical enquiry
• Do they appreciate that some ancient civilizations showed greater advancements than people who lived centuries after them?	• Can they suggest relationships between causes in history? • Can they appreciate how Britain once had an Empire and how that has helped or hindered our relationship with a number of countries today? • Can they trace the main events that define Britain's journey from a mono to a multi-cultural society?	• Can they suggest why there may be different interpretations of events? • Can they suggest why certain events, people and changes might be seen as more significant than others? • Can they pose and answer their own historical questions?

Knowledge, Skills and Understanding breakdown for Geography

Year 6

Geographical Enquiry	Physical Geography	Human Geography	Geographical Knowledge
• Can they confidently explain scale and use maps with a range of scales? • Can they choose the best way to collect information needed and decide the most appropriate units of measure? • Can they make careful measurements and use the data? • Can they use OS maps to answer questions? • Can they use maps, aerial photos, plans and web resources to describe what a locality might be like?	• Can they give extended descriptions of the physical features of different places around the world? • Can they describe how some places are similar and others are different in relation to their human features? • Can they accurately use a 4 figure grid reference? • Can they create sketch maps when carrying out a field study?	• Can they give an extended description of the human features of different places around the world? • Can they map land use with their own criteria? • Can they describe how some places are similar and others are different in relation to their physical features?	• Can they recognise key symbols used on ordnance survey maps? • Can they name the largest desert in the world? • Can they identify and name the Tropics of Cancer and Capricorn as well as the Artic and Antarctic circles? • Can they explain how the time zones work?

Year 6 (Challenging)

• Can they define geographical questions to guide their research? • Can they use a range of self selected resources to answer questions?	• Can they plan a journey to another part of the world which takes account of time zones? • Do they understand the term sustainable development? Can they use it in different contexts?	• Can they explain how human activity has caused an environment to change? • Can they analyse population data on two settlements and report on findings and questions raised?	• Can they name and locate the main canals that link different continents? • Can they name the main lines of latitude and meridian of longitude?

Year 6 : I'm a Year 6 pupil, can you get me out of here?

KS2 Geography:
- use the eight points of a compass, four-figure grid references, symbols and key (including the use of Ordnance Survey maps) to build their knowledge of the United Kingdom and the wider world
- use fieldwork to observe, measure and record the human and physical features in the local area using a range of methods, including sketch maps, plans and graphs, and digital technologies.

WOW: *Take part in an orienteering activity around the school grounds.*

LC1	What would a bird's eye view of your school look like?
LC2	Can you put together a map of the immediate area around your school?
LC3	Can you explain why your *town exists and what would have brought people to live there in the first place and why do people live there today?
LC4	Can you use an OS map, including compass point directions, to help someone plan a route between two local points?
LC5	If you got lost within 50 miles of your home, how would you go about finding your way home?
LC6	From the photographs you have taken of the immediate area, can you create a painting?
LC7	How would you go about planning a trip to a European city to include cost and time?
Ref	As a class could you create an *'Urban' or 'Rural' School* pointing out the features in your locality.

Literacy Link: Research opportunities, especially in LC3 should see children linking to some of their history skills.

Numeracy Link: Huge number of measurement opportunities in this Learning Challenge. LC1, LC2, LC4, LC5, LC7 provide these opportunities.

Creative Art Link: LC6 should provide an opportunity for children to use their water colour or acrylic paint skills to paint a local scene that they have photographed.

Reflection: The reflection should provide a unique challenge. Children will have heard of 'Forest School' and this is their opportunity to create something similar in their locality.

Kensuke's Kingdom   Michael Morpurgo   When you reach me   Rebecca Stead

The Learning Challenge™
CURRICULUM

Year 6 Geography Knowledge, Skills and Understanding

Geographical Enquiry	Physical Geography	Human Geography	Geographical Knowledge
• Can they confidently explain scale and use maps with a range of scales? • Can they choose the best way to collect information needed and decide the most appropriate units of measure? • Can they make careful measurements and use the data? • Can they use OS maps to answer questions? • Can they use maps, aerial photos, plans and web resources to describe what a locality might be like?	• Can they give an extended description of the physical features of different places around the world? • Can they describe how some places are similar and others are different in relation to their human features? • Can they accurately use a 4 figure grid reference? • Can they create sketch maps when carrying out a field study?	• Can they map land use with their own criteria? • Can they describe how some places are similar and others are different in relation to their physical features?	• Can they recognise key symbols used on ordnance survey maps?
Year 6 (Challenging)			
• Can they define geographical questions to guide their research? • Can they use a range of self-selected resources to answer questions?	• Can they plan a journey to another part of the world which takes account of time zones? • Do they understand the term 'sustainable development'? • Can they use it in different contexts?	• Can they explain how human activity has caused an environment to change? • Can they analyse population data on two settlements and report on findings and questions raised?	

The Learning Challenge™
CURRICULUM

Year 6 Art & Design Knowledge, Skills and Understanding

Drawing	Painting	Knowledge	Sketch books
• Can they explain why they have combined different tools to create their drawings? • Can they explain why they have chosen specific drawing techniques?	• Can they explain what their own style is? • Can they use a wide range of techniques in their work? • Can they explain why they have chosen specific painting techniques?	• Can they make a record about the styles and qualities in their work? • Can they say what their work is influenced by? • Can they include technical aspects in their work, e.g. architectural design?	• Do their sketch books contain detailed notes, and quotes explaining about items? • Do they compare their methods to those of others and keep notes in their sketch books? • Do they combine graphics and text based research of commercial design, for example magazines, etc., to influence the layout of their sketch books. • Do they adapt and refine their work to reflect its meaning and purpose, keeping notes and annotations in their sketch books?

Year 6: Will you ever see the water you drink again?

KS2 Geography: Understand the water cycle

WOW: *Show clips of extreme outcomes involving water, eg, waves crashing, rainstorm, waterfall, flood etc.*

LC1	Why is water a major necessity in any village, town or city?
LC2	How does rainwater form in the first place?
LC3	Why do some places go for a long time without rain and others have too much rain?
LC4	How is water used to help provide energy to many places?
LC5	Can you create a moving toy that requires water to power it?
LC6	What happens to the water in our home once it disappears down the sink?
LC7	Which music is associated with water and can you create your own?
Ref	Can you put together a presentation that outlines the water cycle?

Literacy Link: Huge opportunities for children to carry out their own research. LC1 to LC4 offer these opportunities.

Numeracy Link: In LC5 there will be many opportunities for children to use accurate measurement skills

Creative Art Link: LC5 will require children to research, plan, design and make a quality product. The outcome should be quite sophisticated and well made.

Expressive Art Link: Chance in LC7 for children to appraise music before creating their own which should be quite dramatic in capturing different aspects from tiny raindrops to extreme weather storms.

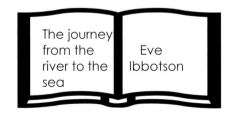

The journey from the river to the sea — Eve Ibbotson

Year 6 Geography Knowledge, Skills and Understanding

Geographical Enquiry	Physical Geography	Human Geography	Geographical Knowledge
• Can they choose the best way to collect information needed and decide the most appropriate units of measure? • Can they make careful measurements and use the data? • Can they use maps, aerial photos, plans and web resources to describe what a locality might be like?	• Can they give an extended description of the physical features of different places around the world? • Can they describe how some places are similar and others are different in relation to their human features?	• Can they give an extended description of the human features of different places around the world? • Can they describe how some places are similar and others are different in relation to their physical features?	• Can they recognise key symbols used on ordnance survey maps? • Can they name the largest desert in the world? • Can they identify and name the Tropics of Cancer and Capricorn as well as the Artic and Antarctic circles?
Year 6 (Challenging)			
• Can they define geographical questions to guide their research? • Can they use a range of self-selected resources to answer questions?	• Do they understand the term 'sustainable development'? Can they use it in different contexts?	• Can they explain how human activity has caused an environment to change? • Can they analyse population data on two settlements and report on findings and questions raised?	• Can they name and locate the main canals that link different continents? • Can they name the main lines of latitude and meridian of longitude?

Year 6 Design Technology Knowledge, Skills and Understanding

Developing, planning and communicating ideas	Working with tools, equipment, materials and components to make quality products	Evaluating processes and products
• Can they use a range of information to inform their design? • Can they use market research to inform plans? • Can they work within constraints? • Can they follow and refine their plan if necessary? • Can they justify their plan to someone else? • Do they consider culture and society in their designs?	• Can they use tools and materials precisely? • Do they change the way they are working if needed?	• How well do they test and evaluate their final product? • Is it fit for purpose? • What would improve it? • Would different resources have improved their product? • Would they need more or different information to make it even better?
Electrical and mechanical components • Can they use different kinds of circuit in their product? • Can they think of ways in which adding a circuit would improve their product?	**Stiff and flexible sheet materials** • Can they justify why they selected specific materials? • Can they work within a budget? • How have they ensured that their work is precise and accurate? • Can they hide joints so as to improve the look of their product?	**Mouldable materials** • Did they consider the use of the product when selecting materials? • Does their product meet all design criteria?

Year 6 Music Knowledge, Skills and Understanding

• Can they refine and improve their work?
• Can they evaluate how the venue, occasion and purpose affects the way a piece of music is created?
• Can they analyse features within different pieces of music?
• Can they compare and contrast the impact that different composers from different times will have had on the people of the time?
• Can they use a variety of different musical devices in their composition? (incl melody, rhythms and chords)
• Do they recognise that different forms of notation serve different purposes?
• Can they use different forms of notation?
• Can they combine groups of beats?

The Learning Challenge™
CURRICULUM

Year 6: Were the Vikings always victorious and vicious?

KS2 History. The Viking and Anglo-Saxon struggle for the kingdom of England
- Viking raids
- Edward the Confessor

WOW: *Visit to Jorvik or a film showing life in a Viking village.*

LC1	Who were the Anglo-Saxons and did they like the Vikings?
LC2	Which region of Britain would you have come under during the Heptarchy?
LC2	Why did the Vikings come to Britain and how did they make the journey?
LC3	What did the Brits learn from the Vikings?
LC4	What was life like for a 11 year old (boy/ girl) Viking?
LC5	How did the Vikings live when they came to Britain?
LC6	How can you create a Viking long boat from a range of materials?
LC7	What did the Vikings eat and could you recreate a Viking meal?
LC8	Reflection: Children to prepare a Viking day when they show others the crafts and skills that the Vikings had.

Literacy Link: Opportunities for children to carry out research in LC1, LC2, LC3, LC4, LC5 and LC7. However, the style of work resulting should look very different.
Opportunities for map work in LC2 and LC3.

Numeracy Link: The way in which the seven regions of the Heptarchy (LC2) were divided up could easily lead to maths work related to area.

Creative Art Link: During LC6 children should design and make a Viking long boat. This follows a period of research in the first instance.

Creative Art Link: During LC7 children should research in the first instance and then design and make a Viking style meal. They should aim to eat this meal on Friday of the week of this LC.

How to train your Dragon	Cressida Cowell

The Saga of Eric the Viking	Terry Jones

The Learning Challenge™
CURRICULUM

Year 6 History Knowledge, Skills and Understanding breakdown for

Chronological understanding	Knowledge and interpretation	Historical enquiry
• Can they say where a period of history fits on a timeline? • Can they place a specific event on a timeline by decade? • Can they place features of historical events and people from past societies and periods in a chronological framework?	• Can they summarise the main events from a specific period in history, explaining the order in which key events happened? • Can they summarise what Britain may have learnt from other countries and civilizations through time gone by and more recently? • Can they describe features of historical events and people from past societies and periods they have studied? • Can they recognise and describe differences and similarities/ changes and continuity between different periods of history?	• Can they look at two different versions and say how the author may be attempting to persuade or give a specific viewpoint? • Can they identify and explain their understanding of propaganda? • Can they describe a key event from Britain's past using a range of evidence from different sources?
Year 6 (Challenging)		
• Do they appreciate that some ancient civilizations showed greater advancements than people who lived centuries after them?	• Can they suggest relationships between causes in history? • Can they trace the main events that define Britain's journey from a mono to a multi-cultural society?	• Can they suggest why there may be different interpretations of events? • Can they suggest why certain events, people and changes might be seen as more significant than others? • Can they pose and answer their own historical questions?

Year 6 Design Technology Knowledge, Skills and Understanding breakdown

Developing, planning and communicating ideas	Working with tools, equipment, materials and components to make quality products	Evaluating processes and products
• Can they use a range of information to inform their design? • Can they use market research to inform plans? • Can they work within constraints? • Can they follow and refine their plan if necessary? • Can they justify their plan to someone else? • Do they consider culture and society in their designs?	• Can they use tools and materials precisely? • Do they change the way they are working if needed?	• How well do they test and evaluate their final product? • Is it fit for purpose? • What would improve it? • Would different resources have improved their product? • Would they need more or different information to make it even better?

Breadth of study

Cooking and Nutrition	Stiff and flexible sheet materials	Mouldable materials
• Can they explain how their product should be stored with reasons? • Can they set out to grow their own products with a view to making a salad, taking account of time required to grow different foods?	• Can they justify why they selected specific materials? • Can they work within a budget? • How have they ensured that their work is precise and accurate? • Can they hide joints so as to improve the look of their product?	• Did they consider the use of the product when selecting materials? • Does their product meet all design criteria?

The Learning Challenge™
CURRICULUM

Year 6: Why was the Islamic Civilization around AD900 known as the 'Golden Age'?

KS2 History. A non European society that provides contrast with British history
- Early Islamic Civilization, including a study of Baghdad in AD 900

WOW: Get children to try and communicate without using pen and paper as they would have done pre the Golden Age.

LC1	What did this 'Golden Age' give the world?
LC2	Who is the Prophet Muhammad and how was he associated with the Golden Age?
LC3	What can you find out about the 'House of Wisdom'?
LC4	What part did the 'Golden Age' have in improving health care?
LC5	What can you discover about the art and culture of the 'Golden Age'?
LC6	How can you make your own paper?
LC7	Why did the 'Golden Age' come to an end?
LC8	Reflection: Create a television documentary to explain to everyone about life in Baghdad in 900AD

Literacy Link: Opportunities exist for children to carry out research in LC1; LC2; LC3 and LC7.
In each case there could be encouragement for children to vary their style of outcomes, ie, presentation, prose, etc.

Numeracy Link: many opportunities for children to work out dates and period of time. In addition, the research work should lead to the need to use tables and charts.

Creative Art Link: LC5 could easily lead to children creating their own pages of manuscript. This could be connected to LC7 where children make their own paper in the first instance.

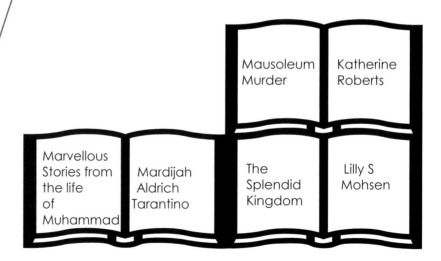

Marvellous Stories from the life of Muhammad

Mardijah Aldrich Tarantino

The Splendid Kingdom

Lilly S Mohsen

Mausoleum Murder

Katherine Roberts

Year 6 History Knowledge, Skills and Understanding breakdown for

Chronological understanding	Knowledge and interpretation	Historical enquiry
• Can they say where a period of history fits on a timeline? • Can they place a specific event on a timeline by decade? • Can they place features of historical events and people from past societies and periods in a chronological framework?	• Can they summarise the main events from a specific period in history, explaining the order in which key events happened? • Can they summarise what Britain may have learnt from other countries and civilizations through time gone by and more recently? • Can they describe features of historical events and people from past societies and periods they have studied? • Can they recognise and describe differences and similarities/ changes and continuity between different periods of history?	• Can they look at two different versions and say how the author may be attempting to persuade or give a specific viewpoint? • Can they identify and explain their understanding of propaganda?
Year 6 (Challenging)		
• Do they appreciate that some ancient civilizations showed greater advancements than people who lived centuries after them?	• Can they suggest relationships between causes in history? • Can they trace the main events that define Britain's journey from a mono to a multi-cultural society?	• Can they suggest why there may be different interpretations of events? • Can they suggest why certain events, people and changes might be seen as more significant than others? • Can they pose and answer their own historical questions?

Year 6 Art & Design Knowledge, Skills and Understanding breakdown

Drawing	Painting	Printing	Sketch books
• Do their sketches communicate emotions and a sense of self with accuracy and imagination? • Can they explain why they have combined different tools to create their drawings? • Can they explain why they have chosen specific drawing techniques?	• Can they explain what their own style is? • Can they use a wide range of techniques in their work? • Can they explain why they have chosen specific painting techniques?	• Can they overprint using different colours? • Do they look very carefully at the methods they use and make decisions about the effectiveness of their printing methods?	• Do their sketch books contain detailed notes, and quotes explaining about items? • Do they compare their methods to those of others and keep notes in their sketch books? • Do they combine graphics and text based research of commercial design, for example magazines etc., to influence the layout of their sketch books. • Do they adapt and refine their work to reflect its meaning and purpose, keeping notes and annotations in their sketch books?

Year 6: Who were the Mayans and what have we learnt from them ?

KS2 History. A non European society that provides contrast with British history
- Mayan civilization around 900AD

WOW: Children to learn about the traditional game 'pok a tok' and recreate it, using resources available to them.

LC1	Who were the Mayans and where did they live?
LC2	What evidence do we have that the Mayans were an advanced civilization?
LC3	What have the Mayan civilization in common with space travel?
LC4	What can we learn from the way they built their pyramids?
LC5	What do we know of the rituals carried out by the Mayan civilization?
LC6	Why was the Sun an important feature in Mayan life?
LC7	What caused the Mayan Civilization to disappear?
LC8	Reflection: Create a television documentary to explain to everyone about the life of the Mayans, focusing on traditions, culture, sport and their knowledge.

Literacy Link: Research opportunities arise in LC1, LC2, LC3, LC5, LC6 and LC7. The main issue is to ensure that the outcomes from the research is different from each LC.
There are several opportunities for pupils to develop their oracy skills, using different talk genre.

Numeracy Link: There are many opportunities for children to work out dates and period of time. In addition, the research work should lead to the need to use tables and charts.

Creative Art Link: LC4 provides opportunities for children to design and make pyramids in the style of the Mayans.

IT Links: The reflection LC provides opportunities for groups of children to present their ideas using their IT skills.

The Mayan Civilization — Elizabeth Scholl

Mayan Civilization Moments in History — Shirley Jordon

The Learning Challenge™
CURRICULUM

Year 6 History Knowledge, Skills and Understanding breakdown

Chronological understanding	Knowledge and interpretation	Historical enquiry
• Can they say where a period of history fits on a timeline? • Can they place a specific event on a timeline by decade? • Can they place features of historical events and people from past societies and periods in a chronological framework?	• Can they summarise the main events from a specific period in history, explaining the order in which key events happened? • Can they summarise what Britain may have learnt from other countries and civilizations through time gone by and more recently? • Can they describe features of historical events and people from past societies and periods they have studied? • Can they recognise and describe differences and similarities/ changes and continuity between different periods of history?	• Can they look at two different versions and say how the author may be attempting to persuade or give a specific viewpoint? • Can they identify and explain their understanding of propaganda?
Year 6 (Challenging)		
• Do they appreciate that some ancient civilizations showed greater advancements than people who lived centuries after them?	• Can they suggest relationships between causes in history? • Can they trace the main events that define Britain's journey from a mono to a multi-cultural society?	• Can they suggest why there may be different interpretations of events? • Can they suggest why certain events, people and changes might be seen as more significant than others? • Can they pose and answer their own historical questions?

The Learning Challenge™
CURRICULUM

Year 6 Design Technology Knowledge, Skills and Understanding breakdown

Developing, planning and communicating ideas	Working with tools, equipment, materials and components to make quality products	Evaluating processes and products
<ul><li>Can they use a range of information to inform their design?</li><li>Can they use market research to inform plans?</li><li>Can they work within constraints?</li><li>Can they follow and refine their plan if necessary?</li><li>Can they justify their plan to someone else?</li><li>Do they consider culture and society in their designs?</li></ul>	<ul><li>Can they use tools and materials precisely?</li><li>Do they change the way they are working if necessary?</li></ul>	<ul><li>How well do they test and evaluate their final product?</li><li>Is it fit for purpose?</li><li>What would improve it?</li><li>Would different resources have improved their product?</li><li>Would they need more or different information to make it even better?</li></ul>

Breadth of study

Stiff and flexible sheet materials
- Can they justify why they selected specific materials?
- Can they work within a budget?
- How have they ensured that their work is precise and accurate?
- Can they hide joints so as to improve the look of their product?

Mouldable materials
- Did they consider the use of the product when selecting materials?
- Does their product meet all design criteria?

Geography and History Learning Challenges

Additional Key Stage 2 examples

These examples have been designed for schools in specific localities or with specific contexts and are provided as a set of ideas.

Consider your context without losing sight of National Curriculum coverage when making adaptations to suit your school and pupils' needs.

Year 3: Which significant events have happened in Stanhope over the past 150 years?

KS2 History: A local history study
- a study of an aspect of history or a site dating from a period beyond 1066 that is significant in the locality.

WOW: *Ask children to visit Ashford Museum and ensure that they see the clock (made by German prisoners of war) and the bell (used to be located in the Industrial school).*

LC1	What secrets does the skyline hold to tell you that Ashford is an old town?
LC2	Why is there a large stone in the ground marked '1877 Industrial School'?
LC3	Where was the prisoner of war camp located in Stanhope?
LC4	What can we find out about the lives of children who attended the workhouse in Willsborough?
LC5	What can a visit to St Mary's Church tell us about the history of Stanhope?
LC6	What happened to most of the children who lived in Ashford during World War 2?
LC7	Reflection: Can you use photographs to create a presentation about Stanhope's recent history?

Creative Art Link: This LC will provide opportunities for children to make sketches of the skyline to include the chimneys and other historical artefacts seen.

Literacy Link: There are several opportunities for research here.
- LC2 – find out about industrial schools;
- LC3 – find out about prisoner of war camps; LC4 – find out about workhouses;
- LC5 – find out about individual children who were evacuated.

Numeracy Links: Opportunities here to find out how long ago things happened; how long people lived; etc.

ICT: Great opportunity here to take photographs and to use them in a presentation about the history of Stanhope.

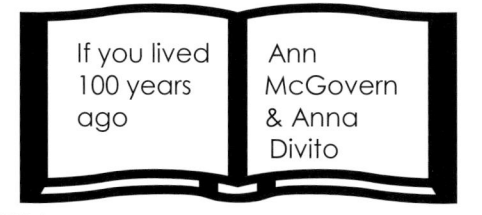

| If you lived 100 years ago | Ann McGovern & Anna Divito |

The Learning Challenge
CURRICULUM

Year 3: How did the Victorian period help to shape the Atherton we know today?

KS2 History: Local History - A study of Local History taking account of a period of history that shaped the locality

WOW: Children to go on a guided walk through a part of Atherton and photograph what was there 100 years ago; between 50 and 100 years ago; and less than 50 years ago.

LC1	What made people come and live in Atherton in the first place?
LC2	When did St. Richard's Church and school open and what can we find out about their history?
LC3	Why does Atherton have a Pitt memorial?
LC4	Has anyone famous ever lived in Atherton?
LC5	How can we capture Atherton's history in art and music?
LC6	What is Enamill and why is it an important part of the history of Atherton?
LC7	Why does Atherton have a railway station and when was it opened?
LC8	Reflection: Children to carry out an IT presentation of the advantages and disadvantages of living in Victorian Atherton

Literacy Link: Opportunities for children to carry out research exist in LC1, LC2, LC3, LC4, LC6 and LC7.

Literacy Link: In LC2 the children will divide into 2 groups with each group researching the history of the school or the history of the Church.

Creative Art Link: In LC5 half the children will use old photographs and create their own images of Atherton based on LS Lowry's style. The other half can look at Atherton today and paint the buildings in the same street as the Lowry group.

Expressive Art Links: Children will perform the music that children would have sung in Victorian times

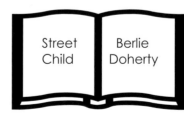

Street Child
Berlie Doherty

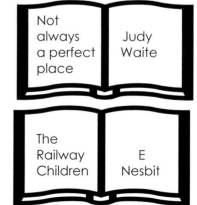

Not always a perfect place
Judy Waite

The Railway Children
E Nesbit

Year 3: Where did all the mills go?

KS2 History: Local History - A study of Local History taking account of a period of history that shaped the locality

WOW: Children to go on a bus ride around Oldham.

LC1	What would you ask the Mayor of Oldham?
LC2	Who are/were the famous people of Oldham?
LC3	What brought people to live in Oldham in the first place?
LC4	How has Oldham changed since your grandparents were little?
LC5	What changes do you know about that are happening now?
LC6	How can you capture Oldham in art which shows its journey through the last 100 years?
LC7	What's so different about Manchester?
LC8	Reflection: How would you go about attracting people to come to live in Oldham?

Literacy Link: Opportunities for children to prepare questions to ask the Mayor in LC1. In LC2 children will be provided with opportunities to carry out research about famous Oldham people.
In LC3 children will need to ask their families what bought their parents or grandparents to Oldham and where did they come from originally.

Creative Art Link: In LC6 children will be provided with opportunities to consider old photographs alongside modern photographs to include the new tramway system and create an abstract work of art as a result.

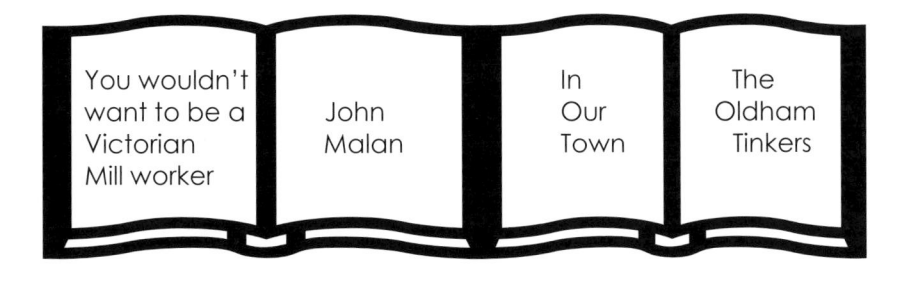

You wouldn't want to be a Victorian Mill worker | John Malan | In Our Town | The Oldham Tinkers

The Learning Challenge
CURRICULUM

Year 4: Why is Canterbury such a 'cool' place to visit?

KS2 History: A local history study
- a study of an aspect of history or a site dating from a period beyond 1066 that is significant in the locality.

WOW: *Visit to Canterbury to include visit to the Cathedral.*

LC1	How would you go about planning to get to Canterbury?
LC2	Why is Canterbury a very important place for Christians?
LC3	Why has Canterbury Cathedral always been a special historical place?
LC4	Why is it said that the ghost of Thomas Beckett roams the cathedral?
LC5	How has the population of Canterbury changed over the centuries?
LC6	Why is 'Thanington Without' so called and what connection does it have with the walled city of Canterbury?
LC7	Reflection: Can you write a guidebook for visitors to Canterbury?

Literacy Link: Children to think of the questions they would ask a pilot from the battle (LC5) or Winston Churchill (LC2).
Research opportunities: Finding out about the spitfire (LC3)and finding out about Dunkirk (LC7)

Geographical Links: Finding out more about the geography of Kent and its strategic position.

Creative Art Link: This LC will see pupils use water colour to recreate a sky and then use accurate sketches to capture the planes in flight.

Numeracy Links: Opportunities here to find out about speed and other attributes of the planes in the battle.

Expressive Arts link: Making use of the music of the period. Pupils could learn to sing some of the familiar songs or make music to accompany the songs.

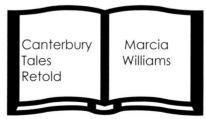

Canterbury Tales Retold   Marcia Williams

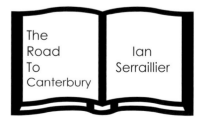

The Road To Canterbury   Ian Serraillier

The Learning Challenge
CURRICULUM

Year 4: Why is Luton a 'cool' place to live and why has the river Lea always been important?

KS2 Geography: understand geographical similarities and differences through the study of human and physical geography of a region of the United Kingdom

WOW: *A bus tour of Luton to take in some notable landmarks*

LC1	Can you think of five or six places in Luton that you would want to show off to a <special visitor>?
LC2	What is so fascinating about Luton airport and why is it so important to the people of Luton?
LC3	Why was the River Lea the original M1?
LC4	How has Luton benefitted from being so close to London?
LC5	How can you capture some of Luton's 'special places' in art?
LC6	Which famous people from history are associated with Luton?
LC7	Reflection: How would you go about attracting people to Luton?

Literacy Link: LC1 provides opportunities for children to research about Luton and then make decisions about where they would like to visit during the bus tour.

LC2 would provide pupils with opportunities to put together a fact file about how Luton airport works. This would include photographs they will have taken on the visit.

LC3 provides ample opportunities for pupils to carry out research based on transporting goods in the Victorian era. (history link)

LC7 provides opportunities for children to create their own guide books or create a TV advert. In each case persuasive language will be required.

Numeracy Links: Measuring how far Luton is from London; costs of holidays (from Luton airport); timetables, etc.

Creative Art Link: LC5 provides opportunities for children to take photographs of famous or notable buildings and then use these photographs to create water colour paintings.

Hats and Headdresses Through history

Fiona McDonald

Hairy MacLary's Hat Trick

Lynley Dodd

The Learning Challenge
CURRICULUM

Year 4: Why is Luton Town known as the 'Hatters'?

KS2 History: A local history study
- a study of an aspect of history or a site dating from a period beyond 1066 that is significant in the locality.

WOW: *Invite a Luton Town player into the classroom*

LC1	What would you ask a Luton Town footballer?
LC2	Why was Luton an ideal place for the manufacturing of hats?
LC3	How have the hats changed over the years?
LC4	What can we find out about the production of hats from our visit to Wardown museum?
LC5	Does anyone still make hats in Luton and what else is Luton now famous for manufacturing?
LC6	Can you design and make a hat suitable for the 21st century?
LC7	Reflection: Can you plan a 'Hatters Day' to involve our school community?

Literacy Link: LC1 provides opportunities for children to think of appropriate questions to ask a visitor.
Research opportunities are provided in a range of ways: finding out about hat manufacturing; changes to fashion; other forms of manufacturing locally.

Numeracy Links: Opportunities for children to consider costs associated with manufacturing of the hats and also the costs of cars, etc.

Creative Art Link: LC6 provides an opportunity for children to design and make a hat which takes account of the older hats but mainly ones that would be considered 'cool' now.

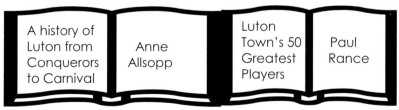

A history of Luton from Conquerors to Carnival — Anne Allsopp

Luton Town's 50 Greatest Players — Paul Rance

The Learning Challenge
CURRICULUM

Year 5: How did the Battle of Britain change World War 2?

KS2 History: A study of an aspect or theme in British history that extends pupils' chronological knowledge beyond 1066, e.g. a significant turning point in British history, e.g. the first railways or the Battle of Britain

WOW: *Start by recreating the warning of the sound of a siren going off.*

LC1	Why is Kent closely associated with the Battle of Britain?
LC2	Who was Churchill and what role did he play in the Battle of Britain?
LC3	What was the Spitfire and why was it so vital in the battle?
LC4	What might the sky have looked like during the battle?
LC5	What can you find out about some of the famous pilots?
LC6	What music do we associate with this period of history?
LC7	Which other landmark war event do we associate with Kent?
LC8	Reflection: Can you recreate what life might have been like for a young child during the Battle of Britain?

Literacy Link: Children to think of the questions they would ask a pilot from the battle (LC5) or Winston Churchill (LC2).
Research opportunities: Finding out about the spitfire (LC3)and finding out about Dunkirk (LC7)

Geographical Links: Finding out more about the geography of Kent and its strategic position.

Creative Art Link: This LC will see pupils use water colour to recreate a sky and then use accurate sketches to capture the planes in flight.

Numeracy Links: Opportunities here to find out about speed and other attributes of the planes in the battle.

Expressive Arts link: Making use of the music of the period. Pupils could learn to sing some of the familiar songs or make music to accompany the songs.

You wouldn't want to be a WW2 pilot	Ian Graham	Battle of Britain	B Asso

The Learning Challenge
CURRICULUM

Year 5: How would you have survived Medieval England?

KS2: Life in 14th-century England, including:
- **Chivalry; the Black Death; the Peasants' Revolt**
- **the later Middle Ages and the early modern period, including:**
- **Chaucer and the revival of learning; Wycliffe's Bible;**
- **Caxton and the introduction of the printing press ; the Wars of the Roses and Warwick the Kingmaker**

WOW: *Children to understand more about chess and relate the pieces to Medieval England.*

LC1	How brave and honest would you have to be to be a knight in Medieval England?
LC2	What do we know about the code of Chivalry amongst knights?
LC3	Is there any connection between 'Ring a ring o'roses' and the Black Death?
LC4	How differently did the rich and poor live in Medieval England?
LC5	How important was religion in the Middle Ages?
LC6	Can you create a board game based around knights and Medieval England?
LC7	Have neighbours always fallen out?
LC8	Reflection: Children to produce a power point presentation on the advantages and disadvantages of being alive in the Medieval period.

Literacy Link: Research opportunities in LC1 and LC2 linked directly to knights and chivalry.
LC3 will allow children to find out about some of the myths associated wit h the Black Death.
LC7 provides opportunities for children to consider the importance of the War of the Roses and link it to other neighbours who have found it difficult to live with each other.

Creative Art Link: In LC6 children will have an opportunity to bring together everything they have learnt about Medieval England and design and create a board game. This will link further the idea of chess which they will have considered at the beginning of the Learning Challenge.

The Children of Winter — Berlie Doherty

Adam of the Road — Elizabeth Janet Gray

The Learning Challenge
CURRICULUM

Year 5: What were the historical implications of Henry VIII's break from the Catholic Church?

KS2 History: A study of an aspect or theme in British history that extends pupils' chronological knowledge beyond 1066, e.g. a significant turning point in British history.

WOW: *Watch TV extracts from 'The Terrible Tudors' from the Horrible Histories and receive a visit from Henry VIII.*

LC1	What would you ask Henry VIII if you met him today?
LC2	How did Henry VIII's decision to break away from the Catholic Church impact on Tudor life and our life today?
LC3	How did the Tudors entertain themselves?
LC4	Which notable events took place during the reign of Elizabeth I?
LC5	Why was the Tudor period often known as the age of 'The Discoveries'?
LC6	Why was Spain our main enemy during the Tudor period?
LC7	If you were quite wealthy, what would your house look like?
LC8	What would an 'everyday' Tudor meal have looked like?
LC9	Reflection: Children to consider what life would have been like as a poor or a wealthy child?

Literacy Link: LC1 - Children to think of the questions they would wish to ask Henry VIII if they met him.
LC2 – Opportunities for research about the formation of the Church of England and its impact on Catholic life in England.
LC4 – Opportunities for distinctive research on the life of Elizabeth I and the notable events that took place during her reign.

Creative Art Link: During LC7, children will design and make their own Tudor house.
During LC8 children will try to make some Tudor recipes.

Expressive Art Link: During LC3 children have to find out about Tudor dances and then perform them as a group.

The Prince & The Pauper — Mark Twain

The time-travellers guide to Tudor London — Natasha Narayan

The Learning Challenge
CURRICULUM

Year 6: To be or not to be, that is the question?

KS2 History:
A study of an aspect or theme in British history that extends pupils' chronological knowledge beyond 1066

WOW: *Ideally, a visit to the reconstructed Globe theatre or a computerised simulation of a visit to the theatre.*

LC1	How would Shakespeare's play have been performed in his day?
LC2	What can you find out about the Globe theatre?
LC3	Who were Shakespeare's most famous characters and what would you ask them if you met them today?
LC4	What sort of people went to the theatre in those days?
LC5	How did Shakespeare cope without a laptop or iPad?
LC6	How can you turn a Shakespearian tragedy into a rap?
LC7	Did Shakespeare really write all those plays?
LC8	Reflection: Working in groups, can you decide on a Shakespearian play and re-enact part of it. Organise a theatre evening, sell tickets and present your work to your parents and friends.

Literacy Link: Clearly there are several literacy links with this Learning Challenge.
Huge opportunity for research exists with LC1, LC2, LC3, LC4 and LC7.
LC7 provides an opportunity for children to consider one of history's most notorious conspiracies.
LC5 provides children with an opportunity to write with old fashion materials.

Expressive Art Link: LC6 provides children with a great opportunity to link modern day music with Shakespeare's couplets.
This is more demanding than might at first be thought.

Reflection: If done properly this could be a wonderful way for a group of children to finish their Primary School life. Children could play different parts to include: actors; producer; technical director, etc.

The Boy, The Bear, The Baron, The Bard — Gregory Rogers

The Learning Challenge
CURRICULUM

Year 6: Why should the world be ashamed of slavery?

KS2 History:
A study of an aspect or theme in British history that extends pupils' chronological knowledge beyond 1066

WOW: *Recreate an auction for children to be sold into slavery.*

LC1	How would you have coped with being sold into slavery?
LC2	Why has slavery existed and what do we know about it?
LC3	What is the link between slavery and discrimination?
LC4	Who are the famous people who have fought against discrimination?
LC5	Can Britain be described as a multi-cultural society?
LC6	How can you capture the emotion associated with slavery in art?
LC7	What rights do children have and does it come with responsibilities?
LC8	Reflection: Can you create a documentary about slavery and its impact on different people's lives?

Literacy Link: Huge opportunities exist for children to debate many issues associated with discrimination in several of the weekly Learning Challenges.
LC4 provides opportunities for children to consider the lives of eminent people such as William Wilberforce.

Creative Art Link: Children could use a range of media to capture images of slavery having first looked at and considered a wide range of photographic and artistic evidence available to them.

Rights and Responsibilities: LC7 takes children into the world of considering what their rights are but also giving a focus on their responsibilities.

Reflection: Huge implications here for pupils' ICT skills, especially in relation to presentation skills.

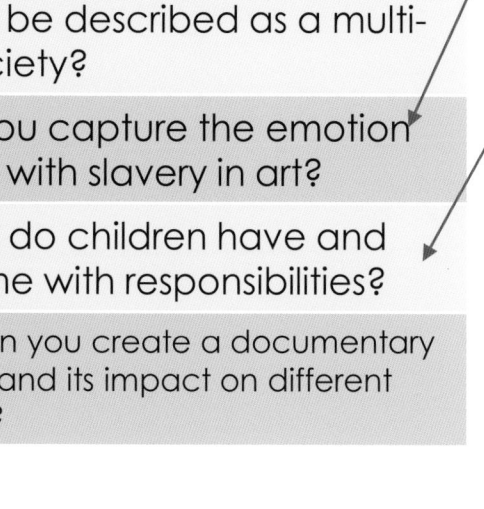

If you lived when there was slavery in America — Anne Kamma

From slave ship to freedom road — Julius Lester & Rod Brown

The Learning Challenge
CURRICULUM

Year 5 or 6: From stone-age man to William the Conqueror: How did Britain change?

KS2 History: To develop a chronologically secure knowledge and understanding of British, local and world history, establishing clear narratives within and across the periods they study.

WOW:. Show illustrations of how life changed from Stone Age to 1066; focus on clothing; shelter; food; weapons, etc.

LC1	What do we know about the first people who lived in Britain?
LC2	How could you cope with communicating without a common language?
LC3	How did the Roman invasion change the life of Britons?
LC4	Who were the famous Romans and what can we find out about them?
LC5	Why did the Romans leave Britain?
LC6	Who were the Anglo-Saxons, and how did they improve Britain?
LC7	When did Christianity first come to Britain and where were the first churches built?
LC8	Where did the Vikings come from and which parts of Britain did they occupy?
LC9	How has crime and punishment changed over the ages?
LC10	Reflection: In groups, can you trace the main changes in the following features of British life from Stone age to 1066: food; art, music and culture; weapons; language; homes?

Literacy Link: LC1: Children to research changes to food; weapons; shelter, etc.
LC2 provides opportunities for children to invent their own ways of communicating. Aim for a demonstration by each group.
LC5 provides children to chart the fall of the Roman Empire.

Creative Art Link: Children should be provided with opportunities to experiment with different art forms according to the period being studied

Expressive Art Link: Similarly, children should be provided with opportunities to experiment with different music, according to the period being studied.

Reflection: Huge implications here for pupils' ICT skills, especially in relation to presentation skills.

The Captive Celt   Terry Dreary   The Saga of Eric the Viking   Terry Jones

The Learning Challenge
CURRICULUM